THE FIVE SIGNS OF A
HEALTHY
Christian

How to be a spiritually healthy and vibrant Christian

FIRST EDITION

Ronald E. Ovitt

GILGAL PUBLISHING
12540 S. 68th Ct.
Palos Heights, IL 60463

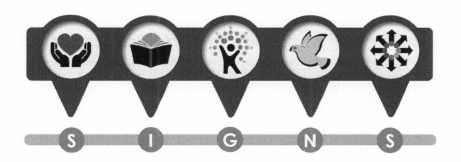

The Five Signs of a Healthy Christian

Printed in the United States of America

Gilgal Publishing
12540 S. 68th Ct.
Palos Heights, IL 60463 708-601-0113

www.empowerministry.org

Contents

Preface

The purpose of this workbook is to help each of us grow in our relationship with the Lord and to be a spiritually healthy and vibrant Christian. This doesn't just happen. It is a deliberate act of the will. We must choose to live for Christ and live a spiritually healthy lifestyle. But why? Does it matter? What is a healthy Christian? How do we get that way?

For some of us, we are new converts and all we really know is the joy of our salvation. While this is wonderful, there hasn't been any significant maturity. We are still babies in Christ. Hopefully, this workbook will create a thirst for more. A deeper walk with God and commitment to spiritual disciplines that will foster growth. Some were born into the faith. This can be good because much is handed down to us from previous generations. However, it is often the case that without revival, the meaning of Christianity gets more and more watered down with each generation. Look at what the Bible says about the Israelites that followed God's miraculous deliverance from Egypt: "After that generation died, another generation grew up who did not acknowledge the LORD or remember the mighty things he had done for Israel" (Judges 2:10).

The Israelites had wandered far from God. Being born into faith in Jehovah, it was hard for them to grasp the privilege that was theirs. They were given the title, "Children of God," and yet for all the ritual and religious practices, they did not know God. They did not remember the stories of the relationship that their predecessors had with Jehovah. Sadly, we can get that way in the church too. So many of us were raised in the church. For some, it becomes the right thing to do—a religious practice. For others, Sunday services are deeply meaningful but not really connected to the rest of their lives on Monday. We know the Bible stories, we know the moral code, and we know the worship songs. But when Monday comes around, our real lives take over. Christianity was never designed for that. God created it as a relationship—a personal walk with God where we become His disciples and live in this world for Him every day. The purpose of this workbook is to help us become healthy in our relationships with God and live for Him every day.

There may have been a time when Christ and the church meant everything to you but life, with all its pressures has taken a toll. You love God and used to serve at church, but somehow the joy has withered away. In burn out, disillusionment, and immersed in busy schedules, perhaps your church attendance has suffered, the Bible has become irrelevant, and everyday life has become a struggle. This workbook is for you.

The fire may still be burning brightly in your heart. When you heard the announcement about this class on being a *Healthy Christian*, you may have said, "Yes, Lord…I want more! Give me more of what I need." Even if you're serving currently at your church, spending time in prayer, participating in Bible studies and devotions, and want to live for God—this workbook is for you, too. There are no perfect Christians. We all need to grow and mature somewhere in our relationship with Christ.

No matter who you are, wherever you are in your walk with God, there is room to mature. Let's work together so we can become *Healthy Christians*.

This workbook is the most effective when used as part of a group study. You will benefit from interaction with others and group discussion. Before you read each lesson, prepare yourself with an open mind and heart. Start with prayer: "God, please speak to my heart and help me live the way you want me to live." Then, whether you have joined a group, answer the group discussion questions.

May God bless you as you participate in this *Healthy Christian* adventure!

THE **FIVE SIGNS** OF A

HEALTHY
Christian

Introduction to the Five Signs

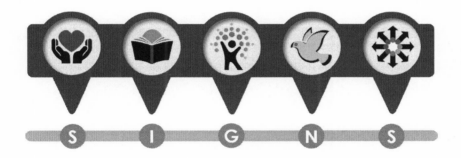

The church can thrive in this generation
and the generations to come. It all begins with
Healthy Christians.

INTRODUCTION

Health is on everyone's mind—our personal health, the health of our nation, the health of our economy. It is all with good reason. When things are unhealthy, bad things start to happen. Yes, this workbook is about the health of the church as an organization and, more specifically, about its individual and collective members. After all, a church is made up of the people that attend.

I've studied church attendance and growth for decades. It doesn't take a national polling group to tell us about the decline in attendance at churches and the ever-changing views on biblical issues. I've attended numerous pastoral conferences where the future of the church is the topic of the day and discussion always includes programs, worship styles, and relevant messages. The impression is that if we get more dynamic programs that attract people, we can pull poor attendance and lack of Bible literacy out of this nosedive. But is that really the solution? That approach has been going on for forty years. I would like to suggest another way.

I believe the church is God's chosen vehicle and that He is vitally interested in its health. But if the church is going to be healthy, if it is going to be a relevant witness in this world, then there must be a revival. But not a revival in methods, programs, and technology, although these are important. I believe the revival needs to be inside us as individuals. The health of the church is only as good as the health of its members. If we are going to be a *Healthy Church* reaching out to our communities with the gospel of Christ, there must be a revival in each and every one of us who call ourselves a Christian. We must be *Healthy Christians*.

The church is alive, but is it well?

Have you stopped by a magazine stand lately and noticed the headlines? There are signs for everything.

- How to know if you are a candidate for a stroke.
- Four indicators that your marriage is in trouble.
- Three habits that lead to financial disaster.

Yes, there are signs that can tell you when you are in danger. But there are also signs that can tell you when you are doing well—key indicators that let you know when you're achieving what you set out to achieve. Articles like *7 Keys to A Healthier You* or *10 Signs of Good Health and Vitality* are designed to be preventative in nature for stopping poor health from happening.

That is the purpose of this workbook. Our goal is for the church to thrive in this generation and the generations to come. But that will only happen if each of us takes full responsibility for our own ✔

spiritual health. This program presents five signs that indicate when a Christian is healthy; signs that if the majority of congregants in your church take seriously, will result in a healthy, vibrant witnessing church!

There are five signs of spiritual health.

There are many relevant indicators of spiritual health and vitality. We use five:

1. Loves Jesus
2. Loves God's Word
3. Emotionally Resilient
4. Led by the Holy Spirit
5. Outwardly Focused

We live by grace and there are no perfect Christians. No matter who we are, we can improve in some area of spiritual health. This workbook provides an effective framework to think about the state of your personal spiritual health. If you stay focused on these five signs of a *Healthy Christian*, pray about each of them, and take even small steps toward achieving the indicators associated with each of them, you will find yourself living a *Healthy Christian* life. How do you know when you are healthy in these areas? We have developed a *Healthy Christian* program with five guided learning lessons— one lesson for each of the five signs. Each lesson includes our *Healthy Christian* survey which lists the behaviors and attributes associated with someone who loves Jesus, loves God's Word, is emotionally resilient, is led by the Holy Spirit, and is outwardly focused.

Explore your personal spiritual vitality.

This workbook is divided into five lessons and each lesson addresses one of the five signs.

INDIVIDUAL EXERCISES

Each lesson includes a personal survey designed to help you identify areas you would like to work on with space provided to create personal goals toward the mental, emotional, and behavior changes needed to increase your spiritual health. Developing new habits to support your goals will help you sustain the change you seek so you can become mature in Christ and live the *Healthy Christian* life God wants you to live.

GROUP DISCUSSIONS

Each lesson also includes a group discussion guide that reviews the information covered in the lesson. If possible, we recommend you take advantage of the benefits of studying *Healthy Christian* with a group so you can share your own thoughts and learn from others.

MEDITATIONS AND AFFIRMATIONS

Bible verses are provided in the Bible Resources section in the back of this book. Verses are grouped into three categories: 1) standard Bible translation verses for your meditation, 2) Bible verses that have been paraphrased, rewritten into the first person for your personal affirmation, and 3) what God believes about you. These Bible verses are companions to each of *The Five Signs of a Healthy Christian* mentioned in this book. Meditate on these scriptures and let God speak to you through His Word. Enjoy being with Him. Listen to the truth God wants you to know through these verses. Sense Him speaking to you through them. This is the biblical truth about you!

1

A Healthy Christian Loves Jesus

I love Jesus with my heart,
my worship, and my actions.

A HEALTHY CHRISTIAN
LOVES JESUS

A *Healthy Christian* loves Jesus. After Jesus died, His disciples went back to fishing. They had their boats and nets and started making a living again. After He resurrected, Jesus appeared to them and had breakfast with them. Jesus took Peter aside and asked him if he wanted to follow Him or planned to go back to his old way of life. He said, "Simon, son of John, do you love me more than these?" He was referring to Peter's fishing nets and boat.

Jesus asks the same of us. Do you love Him enough that you are one of His followers and love Him more than anything else in the whole world?

A *Healthy Christian* loves Jesus. They love Him with their whole hearts. When asked what the greatest commandments were, Jesus said, "You must love the Lord your God with all your heart, all your soul, and all your mind. This is the first and greatest commandment. A second is equally important: Love your neighbor as yourself" (Matthew 22:37-39).

Let's look at loving Jesus a little deeper. How do we love Jesus? We love Him with our hearts, our worship, and our actions.

I love Jesus with my heart.

"One of the Pharisees asked Jesus to have dinner with him, so Jesus went to his home and sat down to eat. When a certain immoral woman from that city heard he was eating there, she brought a beautiful alabaster jar filled with expensive perfume. Then she knelt behind him at his feet, weeping. Her tears fell on his feet, and she wiped them off with her hair. Then she kept kissing his feet and putting perfume on them. When the Pharisee who had invited him saw this, he said to himself, 'If this man were a prophet, he would know what kind of woman is touching him. She's a sinner!' Then Jesus answered his thoughts. 'Simon,' he said to the Pharisee, 'I have something to say to you.' 'Go ahead, Teacher,' Simon replied.

Then Jesus told him this story: 'A man loaned money to two people—500 pieces of silver to one and 50 pieces to the other. But neither of them could repay him, so he kindly forgave them both, canceling their debts. Who do you suppose loved him more after that?' Simon answered, 'I suppose the one for whom he canceled the larger debt.' 'That's right,' Jesus said. Then he turned to the woman and said to Simon, 'Look at this woman kneeling here. When I entered your home, you didn't offer me water to wash the dust from my feet, but she has washed them with her tears and wiped them with her hair. You didn't greet me with a kiss, but from the time I first came in, she has not stopped kissing my feet. You neglected the courtesy of olive oil to anoint my head, but she has anointed my feet with rare perfume. I tell you, her sins—and they are many—have been forgiven, so she has shown me much love. But a person who is forgiven little shows only little love.' Then Jesus said to the woman, 'Your sins are forgiven'" (Luke 7:36-38, 41-50).

Here we see a woman coming to a dinner uninvited, humbling herself at the feet of Jesus and washing His feet with her hair. This was more than a kind gesture. This was an act of worship done with a deep appreciation for who Jesus was. We are given the impression that she heard Christ's teaching and had repented. Her actions were those of someone Jesus called "born again" and she couldn't help but show Him her appreciation. But was what the woman did *that* extreme? If given a chance to be with Jesus, what would you do? When questioned about what the woman was doing Jesus explained that while her sins were many, she was forgiven and because of that, she showed Him great love. He also pointed out that a person who is forgiven for small sins tends to show only a little gratitude and love. How much do *we* love Jesus? Jesus is suggesting that our love for Him is in proportion to what we think He has done for us. The Apostle John explains the love and forgiveness that Jesus gives us:

> "God showed how much he loved us by sending his one and only Son into the world so that we might have eternal life through him. This is real love—not that we loved God, but that he loved us and sent his Son as a sacrifice to take away our sins" (1 John 4:9-10).

It is knowing this love that God has for us that enables us to love Him in return. In fact, John writes in this same passage: "We love because He loved us first" (1 John 4:9-10). Loving Jesus with your heart is more than *knowing* about God's love for you—it is being able to *receive* the love that He gives. It is accepting the fact that even in all your wrongdoing, in all the times you were told or shown that you are unlovable, it did not change God's mind. He loves you. Perhaps you have never received His love and forgiveness for yourself. Ask yourself the following six questions.

1. **Do you believe that God loves you and has a wonderful plan for your life?** Consider the following verses from the Bible.

   "God so loved the world that He gave His one and only Son, that whoever believes in him shall not perish, but have eternal life" (John 3:16, *NIV*).

   [Christ speaking] "I came that they might have life and might have it abundantly [that it might be full and meaningful]" (John 10:10).

   If these verses are true, why aren't most people experiencing God's love and abundant life?

2. **Do you believe that by your own choice you have rebelled against God resulting in wrongful behavior?**

"All have sinned and fall short of the glory of God" (Romans 3:23).

Even though we were created to have fellowship with God, we chose to go our own independent way, and fellowship with God was broken. Whether it is a deliberate wrongdoing or doing nothing because of an attitude of indifference, this is evidence of what the Bible calls sin.

3. **Do you realize that the result of your own rebellion toward God in these wrongful attitudes and behavior (sin) has separated you from God?**

"The wages of sin is death [spiritual separation from God]" (Romans 6:23).

A great gulf separates us from God. We can try to reach God and the abundant life through our own efforts, but they just aren't good enough. We are destined to fail. We need a relationship with God. We need to become His child. A good life, philosophy, or religion just isn't enough.

4. **Do you believe that Jesus Christ's death was for your wrongdoing?**

"God demonstrates His own love toward us, in that while we were yet sinners, Christ died for us" (Romans 5:8).

He created a way for you to become spiritually alive through His death on the cross. This was so you could become a new person, "born again," alive to God, and living as His child.

5. **Do you understand that knowing about Christ is not enough?**

You must individually receive Jesus Christ as Savior and Lord; then you can know and experience God's love and plan for your life.

"As many as received him, to them he gave the right to become children of God, even to those who believe in His name" (John 1:12).

6. **Have you personally, through prayer, invited Jesus Christ to forgive you and make you a new Christian?**

You can be born again and become His child by simply accepting His invitation to receive Him as the God of your choice, the God of your life and the Forgiver of all your sins.

It is not enough to simply say yes to what you are reading. It is more than a mental assent. Repentance is turning away from one thing and turning toward another. You must sincerely turn away from yourself and turn toward Christ, inviting Him to come into your life, to forgive all of your sins, and to make you what He wants you to be. This is more than an emotional experience; it is an act of your will.

Prayer is simply talking to God. The good news is that right now you can receive Christ into your life through prayer. God knows your heart and is not as concerned with your words as He is with the attitude of your heart. The following is a suggested prayer that you can say to God. Please read it. If it expresses your desire, pray it out loud to God. He is here; He will hear you.

> "Lord Jesus, I need You. Thank You for making a way that I can become a child of God. Thank You for dying on the cross in my place so I could be forgiven of all that I have done wrong. I come now and give you my life. I give you my heart and invite you to be the ruler of my life. Come into me, make me a Christian right now. I want to be born again right now."

If you sincerely prayed this prayer, God came into your life and has forgiven you and made you His child! Respond to Him now in prayer by saying: "Thank You for forgiving my sins and giving me eternal life. Take control of my life. Please make me a new person, the kind of person You want me to be."

Share what has happened with your pastor or someone that you trust spiritually. They will want to know so they can celebrate with you.

Jesus created you and me as an object of His love. We are lovable because He created us that way. He loves us for who we are, and nothing can separate us from that love. It is a deep-felt expression of gratitude for the unconditional love that He has for us. Yes, it is knowing the depth of our own depravity but only in light of the height of His own love and forgiveness for us. It is an emotional knowing that we don't deserve His forgiveness, but He gives it to us anyway. This leads us to love Jesus with our worship.

I love Jesus with my worship.

Worship is the expression of love and honor that we give to Jesus. The dictionary defines it as "reverent honor and homage paid to God, a sacred personage, or to any object regarded as sacred." Revelation is the last book in the Bible. In it, the Apostle John tells about a vision he had of the end times. He writes about Jesus sitting on the throne of God and receiving worship from elders, angels, and all living creatures.

"I heard the voices of thousands and millions of angels around the throne and of the living beings and the elders. And they sang in a mighty chorus: 'Worthy is the Lamb who was slaughtered to receive power and riches and wisdom and strength and honor and glory and blessing.' And then I heard every creature in heaven and on earth and under the earth and in the sea. They sang: 'Blessing and honor and glory and power belong to the one sitting on the throne and to the Lamb forever and ever.' And the four living beings said, 'Amen!' And the twenty-four elders fell down and worshiped the Lamb" (Revelation 5:11-14).

In Revelation 5, we see the proclamation that Jesus is truly worthy of everything of worth we could ever give Him. Our praise, adoration, gratitude, all the power in the world, all the riches, all the strength, all the wisdom, all the glory and all the blessing would not even begin to express the glory of who He is. He is the one who created all the galaxies, who formed life, who thought up eternity. He is worthy of all the world has. He is worthy of our devotion, servitude and our very life. It is in beginning to comprehend all of this that worship flows out of our being.

No wonder they sang songs of the merit of Christ with all their hearts. No wonder they bowed down before Him. They knew that He was worthy. They understood His sacrifice and what it meant to them. Likewise, when we begin to understand what Christ has done for us, we can't help but worship Him. When we realize that being *born again* means that we are a new person with the Holy Spirit residing in our lives—that His sacrifice on the cross means we are truly forgiven of all our wrongdoings—we can't help but worship. When we give ourselves to Him and He begins to lead our lives and becomes personal to us, we cannot help but worship. We, too, can join in with those in Revelation 5 and come to worship Jesus with songs that glorify Him. We, too, can come with prayers of thanksgiving. We, too, can express our gratitude with shouts of praise and adoration. This is worship. It is when we take time to give Him praise, thanksgiving, and adoration. Worship is recognizing Him as Lord and giving Him our life; living for Him. This takes us to the third way to love Jesus. We love Jesus with our actions.

I love Jesus with my actions.

Jesus said if we love Him, we should keep His commandments. In the book of Mathew, Jesus responds to a question about commandments.

"And one of them, a lawyer, asked him a question to test him. 'Teacher, which commandment in the law is the greatest?' He said to him, 'You shall love the Lord your God with all your heart, and with all your soul, and with all your mind. This is the greatest and first commandment. And a second is like it: You shall love your neighbor as yourself. On these two commandments hang all the law and the prophets'" (Matthew 22:35-40).

11

The first part of Jesus' answer was from the Shema. To quote the Shema was specifically commanded in Torah. It is the oldest fixed daily prayer in Judaism, recited morning and night since ancient times. It states that we are to love God, not only with our hearts but with our souls and minds as well. The second part Jesus added was that we are to love our neighbor as we love ourselves. Together this is both an inward and outward expression of our love for Christ. It is significant that Christ added the second part. It is in loving others that we truly express our love for God. The Apostle John wrote it this way: "If someone says, 'I love God,' but hates a fellow believer, that person is a liar; for if we don't love people we can see, how can we love God, whom we cannot see?" (1 John 4:20).

Saying we love God without loving others is hypocrisy. James points this out:

> "Suppose you see a brother or sister who has no food or clothing, and you say, 'Good-bye and have a good day; stay warm and eat well' but then you don't give that person any food or clothing. What good does that do? So, you see, faith by itself isn't enough. Unless it produces good deeds, it is dead and useless" (James 2:15-17).

James could have just as easily substituted the word *love* for *faith*. What good is it to say we love God when our actions are not an expression of that love? Loving others is the expression of our love for Christ.

Paul also admonishes us to live out our love for Christ. He says that we need to present our body a living sacrifice: "And so, dear brothers and sisters, I plead with you to give your bodies to God because of all he has done for you. Let them be a living and holy sacrifice—the kind he will find acceptable. This is truly the way to worship him" (Romans 12:1). Paul is saying that we should be living our whole lives in service to Christ. Our love for Christ is expressed in the way we live. What we do, say, and think should be an expression of love and worship for Christ.

A *Healthy Christian* loves Jesus. They love Him with their hearts, their worship, and their actions.

INDIVIDUAL EXERCISE
A Healthy Christian Loves Jesus

PART 1: SELF-ASSESSMENT

Read each statement below and rate yourself according to the frequency in which that statement is true about you. Be honest with yourself. This is not a pass/fail quiz; it is simply a measuring tool to see where you are in your Christian walk as it relates to **loving Jesus**. Don't be afraid to admit that there are some areas where you need to improve. Admitting and committing to change is the way we become and stay spiritually healthy.

I know Jesus as my Savior who has forgiven me of all my wrongdoing.
☑ yes ☐ I think so ☐ not sure ☐ no

I come prepared to meet God on Sunday mornings. ~I'm supposed to be prepared?~
☐ regularly ☐ often ☐ sometimes ☐ no

I listen to Christian music throughout the week. ~I play Christian~
☐ regularly ☐ often ☐ sometimes ☐ no ~91.9? where? Majesty Quartet? Go over CD's.~

I keep a joyful spirit of praise. ~Praise + be raised.~
☐ regularly ☐ often ☐ sometimes ☐ no

I tell God how much I love Him.
☐ regularly ☐ often ☐ sometimes ☐ no

I have a devotional time. ~Print Ovitt Devotions Put in 3ring~
☐ regularly ☐ often ☐ sometimes ☐ no

I express my love for God by helping and loving others.
☐ regularly ☐ often ☐ sometimes ☐ no

PART 2: HEALTHY CHRISTIAN ACTION PLAN

After you complete the self-assessment, pray and ask God about areas you need to work on. Read the following commitment statement and identify personal goals that will help you achieve **loving Jesus** more. Record your goals and monitor your progress as you work toward achieving them. Consider sharing your goals with someone who will support you in your *Healthy Christian* action plan.

Commitment

I commit myself to improving my Christian health by taking the following action steps: I commit myself to improving my Christian health by taking the following action steps:

1. _I listen to Christian music. How?_
    1. _Joni CD's + book_   3. _Play Piano_
    2. _Go thru all CD's + have available_
2. _I have a joyful spirit of Praise_
    Play joyful Praise on Piano + Sing words
    From Bible
    Arise with Praise first thing
3. _I confess, repent, thank. Phil 4 ∴ I Love You_
    Must understand what Christ has + is doing

Bible Verse Resources

Review the Bible resource section in the back of this book. Select two verses that speak to you about **loving Jesus**. Let God speak to you through His Word. Enjoy being with Him. Listen to the truth God wants you to know through these verses. Sense Him speaking to you through them. Claim this biblical truth about you!

1. _____
2. _____

4. Devotional Time Ovi tt
5. Express love by helping + loving others
    Ask Judy Vanderw.

GROUP EXERCISE
A Healthy Christian Loves Jesus

Please review the following questions before you meet for group discussion or move on to the next lesson.

DISCUSSION 1

"One of the Pharisees asked Jesus to have dinner with him, so Jesus went to his home and sat down to eat. When a certain immoral woman from that city heard he was eating there, she brought a beautiful alabaster jar filled with expensive perfume. Then she knelt behind him at his feet, weeping. Her tears fell on his feet, and she wiped them off with her hair. Then she kept kissing his feet and putting perfume on them. When the Pharisee who had invited him saw this, he said to himself, 'If this man were a prophet, he would know what kind of woman is touching him. She's a sinner!' Then Jesus answered his thoughts. 'Simon,' he said to the Pharisee, 'I have something to say to you.' 'Go ahead, Teacher,' Simon replied. Then Jesus told him this story: 'A man loaned money to two people—500 pieces of silver to one and 50 pieces to the other. But neither of them could repay him, so he kindly forgave them both, canceling their debts. Who do you suppose loved him more after that?' Simon answered, 'I suppose the one for whom he canceled the larger debt.' 'That's right,' Jesus said. Then he turned to the woman and said to Simon, 'Look at this woman kneeling here. When I entered your home, you didn't offer me water to wash the dust from my feet, but she has washed them with her tears and wiped them with her hair. You didn't greet me with a kiss, but from the time I first came in, she has not stopped kissing my feet. You neglected the courtesy of olive oil to anoint my head, but she has anointed my feet with rare perfume. I tell you, her sins—and they are many—have been forgiven, so she has shown me much love. But a person who is forgiven little shows only little love.' Then Jesus said to the woman, 'Your sins are forgiven'" (Luke 7:36-38, 41-50).

Was it simple cultural practice, love, or something else that motivated the woman to wash Jesus' feet?

She knew her sins were many, + she was amazed, relieved, overcome w great joy that her sins are forgiven — that she doesn't is not sentence justly to hell as punishment. Her sins were against others but also against God. She realized He had great LOVE for her

How did she express her love for Him? _Honoring Him She could not repay Him God does not demand her payment but She rightly deserved Gods wrath Holy wrath but Jesus went to the cross + took God's wrath that was directed to me Foot wash_

① washed feet too wiped hair
② Greet w a kiss
③ Anointed feet feet w oil perfume
believe + receive

God Holy wrath   15   →   _me_

_4 Jc 11_   _cross_ → _me_

Blood
it of I accept

Why did Jesus share the story about the two men in debt?

To acknowledge that yes I know who she is & the many sins she has committed. Story shows her great love is the same for all BUT the receiver appreciates it more if the weight of their sin is heavier than most → the lifting of sin is a great blessing relief Death to LIFE

In what ways can we love Jesus like the woman did?

Realize *MUST KNOW the seriousness of SIN*
" # have sins revealed
" KNOW penalty for sin
" The humble self confess repent in thankful love to His overwhelming LOVE
LOVE greater love for them
deeper ree of SIN

DISCUSSION 2

"God showed how much he loved us by sending his one and only Son into the world so that we might have eternal life through him. This is real love—not that we loved God, but that he loved us and sent his Son as a sacrifice to take away our sins" (1 John 4:9-10).

According to this passage how did God express His love for us? *by sending His Son so we have eternal life of "knowing" God & His Son John 17:3*

True love for Jesus comes out of what (motivation?) *See p 11 look #*

He loves

16

DISCUSSION 3

"I heard the voices of thousands and millions of angels around the throne and of the living beings and the elders. And they sang in a mighty chorus: 'Worthy is the Lamb who was slaughtered— to receive power and riches and wisdom and strength and honor and glory and blessing.' And then I heard every creature in heaven and on earth and under the earth and in the sea. They sang: 'Blessing and honor and glory and power belong to the one sitting on the throne and to the Lamb forever and ever.' And the four living beings said, 'Amen!' And the twenty-four elders fell down and worshiped the Lamb" (Revelation 5:11-14).

How do you describe worship? _____
_____
_____
_____
_____
_____
_____
_____

In the above Bible passage, how did they worship Christ? _____
_____
_____
_____
_____
_____
_____
_____

In what ways can we worship Jesus? _____
_____
_____
_____
_____
_____
_____
_____
_____
_____

DISCUSSION 4

Jesus said that if we love Him, we'll keep God's commandments. In the book of Matthew, Jesus defines these commandments: "And one of them, a lawyer, asked him a question to test him: 'Teacher, which commandment in the law is the greatest?' He said to him, 'You shall love the Lord your God with all your heart, and with all your soul, and with all your mind. This is the greatest and first commandment. And a second is like it: You shall love your neighbor as yourself'" (Matthew 22:35-39).

How do we love God with all our hearts? _____

_____

_____

_____

_____

_____

How do we love God with all our souls? _____

_____

_____

_____

_____

_____

How do we love God with all our minds? _____

_____

_____

_____

_____

_____

What did Jesus mean when he said we should love our neighbors as ourselves? _____

_____

_____

_____

_____

_____

_____

DISCUSSION 5

Paul admonishes us to present our body a living sacrifice: "And so, dear brothers and sisters, I plead with you to give your bodies to God because of all he has done for you. Let them be a living and holy sacrifice—the kind he will find acceptable. This is truly the way to worship him" (Romans 12:1).

In what way do we give our bodies to Christ as a sacrifice? _____
_____
_____
_____
_____
_____
_____

DISCUSSION 6

"Suppose you see a brother or sister who has no food or clothing, and you say, 'Good-bye and have a good day; stay warm and eat well' but then you don't give that person any food or clothing. What good does that do? So, you see, faith by itself isn't enough. Unless it produces good deeds, it is dead and useless" (James 2:15-17).

In this passage, James is talking about faith. Faith without action is dead. We could also say that love without action is dead. We can say we love Jesus, but our actions will tell others whether we really love Him. What kind of actions speak loudly and say that we love God? _____
_____
_____
_____
_____
_____
_____
_____

DISCUSSION 7

Share one of the verses you selected from the Bible Verse Resources section that spoke to you about **loving Jesus**. How is this verse meaningful to you? _____
_____
_____
_____
_____
_____
_____

2

A Healthy Christian Loves God's Word

I love God's Word by reading it,
studying it, and applying it to
the way I live.

A HEALTHY CHRISTIAN
LOVES GOD'S WORD

Another sign of a *Healthy Christian* is that they love the Bible, God's written Word. This is more than simply knowing about it. It is understanding that in the reading and meditating on it there is a link established between you and God. It nourishes your soul. It gives you direction in life and comfort when needed. It becomes a part of you and you end up loving the time you spend in it. That happened to me.

When I was eleven years old I came to know Christ as my Savior. My father, mother, twin brother and I all went forward at an altar call at the same time. We had previously never gone to church. One day, a young pastor knocked on our front door and invited us to attend a small church he was starting. My father decided to take us. Soon after we began attending, the momentous Sunday came. He preached the gospel message and we responded. I didn't know my whole family was going forward. It was only after I was at the altar, I noticed that they were there, too. Not having gone to church as a family and without a religious background, this was a significant change for us. I remember shortly after that Sunday, my dad challenged me to read the New Testament, making it a race to see who would finish first. I don't remember who won. All I know is that I was mesmerized as I read the Bible. At that young age, God was speaking to my heart. I loved the life of Jesus and was inspired by Paul's writings. I fell in love with God's Word. Ever since that day I have looked to the Bible for guidance, wisdom, assurance, comfort, strength, and God's leading. I love God's Word, the Bible.

Like me, Timothy was a young child when he fell in love with the scriptures they had at that time. Later he grew up to become Paul the Apostle's disciple. In a letter addressed to Timothy, Paul writes:

> "But you must remain faithful to the things you have been taught. You know they are true, for you know you can trust those who taught you. You have been taught the holy Scriptures from childhood, and they have given you the wisdom to receive the salvation that comes by trusting in Christ Jesus. All scripture is inspired by God and is useful to teach us what is true and to make us realize what is wrong in our lives. It corrects us when we are wrong and teaches us to do what is right. God uses it to prepare and equip his people to do every good work" (2 Timothy 3:14-17).

In this passage, we see the reason we need to read God's Word, study it, and apply it. Look how significant this is to our lives! According to the text, the Bible is like a journey book with maps and helpful commentary. In this case, it is the journey of life.

The Bible lets us know which trail we should take (teaches us what is true); when we are off the trail (makes us realize what is wrong in our lives); shows us how to get back on the trail (corrects us when we are wrong); and shows us how to stay on the trail (teaches us to do what is right). God uses the Word to help us get ready (prepares us) for ministry and gives us everything we need (equips us) to do it. There are three ways in which we love God's Word. We love God's Word by reading it, studying it, and applying it.

I love God's Word by reading it.

Loving God's Word is more than believing that it is the Word of God. Many Christians believe that but never read it. Yes, they know about the Bible. They know the stories taught in Sunday School. They read the verses on the screen during the sermons on Sunday. But the sad truth is that a majority of the people in the pew barely read it. Each year the Barna Group surveys the Bible reading habits of people in the church. In 2016 they surveyed 14,000 people and found that 27% of church members never read the Bible at all; 31% only read it one to four times a year; and 7% read it once a month. That is 65% of Christians barely reading the Bible.

When reading about this, Ed Stetzer, president of LifeWay Research commented, "You can follow Christ and see Christianity as your source of truth, but if that truth does not permeate your thoughts, aspirations, and actions, you are not fully engaging the truth. God's Word is truth, so it should come as no surprise that reading and studying the Bible are still the activities that have the most impact on growth in this attribute of spiritual maturity. As basic as that is, there are still numerous churchgoers who are not reading the Bible regularly. You simply won't grow if you don't know God and spend time in God's Word."

Although the same survey pointed out that 27% of Christians do read the Bible every day, that is still less than one-third of the church. If the church is to be healthy, we need a revival about reading God's Word.

HOW TO READ GOD'S WORD

"Oh, the joys of those who do not follow the advice of the wicked, or stand around with sinners, or join in with mockers. But they delight in the law of the Lord, meditating on it day and night" (Psalms 1:1-2).

"Oh, how I love your instructions! I think about them all day long" (Psalms 119:97).

Reading the Bible is different than reading a newspaper article. It's more like a textbook—the Holy Book where you come to be inspired, sense the presence of God, and hear His voice. You want to understand what God is trying to say to you. You want to listen to specific instruction, encouragement, guidance, and correction. This comes from meditating on it. A prayerful request asking God to speak to you from His Word before you read will help tune your heart to hear God's voice.

BENEFITS OF READING GOD'S WORD

Perhaps many are not reading the Bible because they don't appreciate its importance. After all, we tend to do things that benefit us. Understanding why reading the Bible is important will help you develop a love for God's Word and stay disciplined in reading it.

Speaks to us about living. "People do not live by bread alone; rather, we live by every word that comes from the mouth of the Lord" (Deuteronomy 8:3).

Gives us understanding and direction. "Your word is a lamp to guide my feet and a light for my path" (Psalms 119:105).

Returns us to joy, makes us wise, and gives us insight into living. "The instructions of the Lord are perfect, reviving the soul. The decrees of the Lord are trustworthy, making wise the simple. The commandments of the Lord are right, bringing joy to the heart. The commands of the Lord are clear, giving insight for living" (Psalm 19:7-8).

Gives us hope and encouragement. "And the scriptures give us hope and encouragement as we wait patiently for God's promises to be fulfilled" (Romans 15:4).

Guides us in teaching each other. "Let the word of Christ dwell in you richly, teaching and admonishing one another in all wisdom" (Colossians 3:16).

Helps us believe in Jesus. "The disciples saw Jesus do many other miraculous signs in addition to the ones recorded in this book. But these are written so that you may continue to believe that Jesus is the Messiah, the Son of God, and that by believing in him you will have life by the power of his name" (John 20:30-31). Also: "These things I have written unto you that believe in the name of the Son of God, that ye may know that ye have eternal life and that ye may believe in the name of the Son of God" (1 John 5:13).

Helps us discern the truth. "For the word of God is living and powerful and sharper than any two-edged sword, piercing even to the dividing asunder of soul and spirit, and of the joints and marrow, and is a discerner of the thoughts and intents of the heart" (Hebrews 4:12).

HOW AND WHEN TO READ GOD'S WORD

There is a temptation to believe that God is pleased with the quantity of our reading. While we should read enough to speak to our hearts, we don't have to lock ourselves into reading for hours a day. It is better to meet with God, ask Him if there is anything He wants you to know, and then read a Bible passage and meditate on it. You can always spend more time, but to make this a daily habit you need to be able to fit it into the time you have allowed.

Have a plan. We all have good intentions but having a systematic, organized approach to reading the Bible will help you stay on track and be consistent. There are also many Bible reading plans online. Do some research, ask others for suggestions, and find a plan that best suits you.

Be prayerful. Regardless of the plan, the goal is not just to read, but to pray and ask God to speak to your heart. Ask yourself what the verses are saying and what they are saying to you personally. Let them speak to your heart and feel free to talk to God about it.

Be realistic. This is an important consideration. It does no good to be faithful for a week and then drop out. Choose a time when you will be undisturbed and not bothered while you take the time to read, pray and meditate. Many people set their alarm earlier and read and meditate first thing in the morning. Others pick another time during the day. The main thing is to set aside a time where you won't be rushed, bothered, distracted or tempted to do other things.

We love God's Word by reading it. We also love it by studying the Bible.

I love God's Word by studying it.

There is a difference between reading for devotional input from God and studying the Bible to better understand it. Both should be an integral part of the believer's life. Why study? The Apostle Paul explained it to his young disciple Timothy this way: "Be a good worker, one who does not need to be ashamed and who correctly explains the word of truth" (2 Timothy 2:15). This verse applies to us today. The Bible consists of sixty-six individual books with different authors, written at different times, and from various geographic areas. The meaning of words and phrases often change from culture to culture and through multiple generations. We can gain a better understanding of the true meaning of the text if we know about its authorship, original language, historical background, and cultural meaning.

There is no end to the number of books about the Bible and various biblical topics. You could study ten hours a day for the rest of your life and not put a dent in the number of materials available. This is not about becoming a biblical scholar. But like anything, if you are going to become involved at all, there are basic topics you should investigate and pursue.

CHRISTIAN DOCTRINE: THE FOUNDATIONS OF OUR FAITH

The importance of essential Christian doctrine can hardly be overstated. Christian doctrine is the foundation on which the gospel of Jesus Christ rests. From His deity to the eschatological certainty that He will appear a second time to judge the living and the dead, essential Christian doctrine is foundational to the gospel. Hank Hanegraaff, the author of *The Complete Bible Answer Book*, is so passionate about inscribing Christian doctrines on the hearts of believers that he organized them around an acronym:

D	Deity of Christ
O	Original Sin
C	Canon
T	Trinity
R	Resurrection
I	Incarnation
N	New Creation
E	End Times

CHURCH DOCTRINE: WHAT WE BELIEVE AND WHY

A great place to start is with your church's Doctrinal Statement. This is a document that shares what your church and its denomination believe about vital doctrinal issues. This will give you a good foundation from which to build your biblical understanding.

Creeds and catechisms. Over the centuries, the church has taught doctrine through what is called *catechisms*—a summary of doctrine prepared by denominational scholars to serve as a learning introduction to Christian children and adult converts. This form of education typically uses questions followed by answers to be memorized. Such programs are used throughout the denomination in the systematic instruction of its congregants. The most common Creed is the Apostle's Creed. This is an easy to learn creed that capsulizes basic doctrinal beliefs of the church. The famous Heidelberg Catechism, written in 1563, is a remarkably warm-hearted and personalized confession of faith and a great way to learn the teachings of the church.

Scholarly works. There are many books, teachers, websites, and radio programs to choose from when it comes to doctrine. However, not all teachers teach the same thing. There are many theologians and teachers that have strayed from the central teachings of the Bible. Before pursuing Bible institutes or seminaries and doctrine-based study materials, consider checking with your pastoral staff to verify that it is a reliable source. They have been commissioned by God to care for your soul and would be happy to lead you to sources that support your own church's doctrinal view.

APOLOGETICS: DEFENSE OF THE CHRISTIAN FAITH

Apologetics is a branch of Christianity that defends the authority of God's Word, the character of God, and Christianity as a whole. Why should anyone place their faith in Jesus Christ—a man who lived over two thousand years ago? There have certainly been many different answers to this question throughout this history of Christianity. *Christian Apologetics* is both the science and art of answering this question by using reasons and evidence. Apologetics uses the Bible to explore and explain the riches of the truth of Christianity, engaging both skeptics and believers in carefully assessing the evidence that points to Christ as our Creator and Redeemer. There are many teachers, books, and seminars that offer you an opportunity to learn how to explain your faith. As with all endeavors, if you're not sure where an author, institution, or organization stands on Christian beliefs, seek the advice of your pastoral staff.

CONTEMPORARY CHRISTIAN LIVING: CONNECTING THE BIBLE TO REAL LIFE SITUATIONS

Contemporary Christians face many lifestyle issues, such as marriage, finances, morality, parenting, and schools. Have you ever wondered, "How do I make the Bible relevant to my daily life?" When reading the Bible, you can make a biblical text relevant by applying it to the way you live. Connecting the Bible to real-life situations is simply our response to and action taken following our hearing of God's Word. It is the call to "go and do likewise." This call consists of two parts—our internal response and our external action. Our internal response is the heartfelt desire and intellectual decision to act on God's Word; our external action is the fulfillment of that desire and decision. One side alone of the response-and-action equation is not sufficient for application; without a genuine internal response our external action may be misguided, and without an authentic external action our internal response may prove ineffective. The application of a biblical text affects our individual lives, of course. But it often also extends to the corporate life of communities, societies, and institutions. As salt preserves food and light penetrates the darkness, practical action preserves health and illumines the conscience of a society.

Essentially, we are called to be changed and to help change communities, societies, and institutions that do not live in accord with God's shalom—His love, grace, and peace. Research on your own or check with other trusted Christians and your pastoral staff for their recommendations on resource materials, webinars, small group studies, and books available on the topics you're interested in studying.

WHAT ARE SOME WAYS TO STUDY THE BIBLE?

In Proverbs, Solomon encourages us to get wisdom, and with wisdom, get understanding. In reading the Bible, you will get wisdom. But by studying, you can get a deeper understanding. There are more learning options today than ever before. There are courses and books available on doctrine, apologetics, contemporary Christian living, history, archeology, language, biblical interpretation, and difficult questions and answers. Some of the reasons for studying these topics include gaining a knowledge of what the text meant in the author's culture, for our personal edification, to help teach others, to gain a better understanding of Jesus and His mission, to know God better, and to help us avoid theological error. All of these are excellent reasons to pursue in-depth Bible study that will help us grow spiritually.

Instructor-led training. This type of training is facilitated by an instructor either online or in a classroom setting. Instructor-led training allows for learners and instructors or facilitators to interact and discuss the training material, either individually or in a group setting. Students may opt to enroll in credit or non-credit courses, depending on their educational goals.

Self-study learning. There is a multitude of excellent printed and digital study guides designed to help students understand specific aspects of the Bible.

Commentaries. Commentaries are scholarly books that explain biblical passages and help you understand the meaning of the passage you study. While commentaries used to be largely available to academic biblical scholars, they are now fairly common in Bible study software. Also, if you happen to live near a Christian seminary, you might look into accessing their library for more in-depth research, as they tend to have numerous commentaries available. A commentary is fairly simple to use. If you have a question about a particular Bible passage, you consult the relevant Bible commentary and look up the passage and read what the author has said about it.

Study Bibles. A study Bible is indispensable when it comes to addressing most common questions you will have. While a study Bible is not essential to in-depth Bible study, it will help immensely by providing what is essentially a mini-commentary on various passages you encounter.

Bible dictionaries. Formatted like an encyclopedia with short articles arranged in alphabetical order, with a Bible dictionary you can research historical background and cultural context. You can use it to learn about people, places, and what a word or phrase meant at the time of the author.

Word studies. Word studies are one of the basic tools of Bible study. If you want to understand the author's intended meaning, you need to understand the words he chose in his original language. With today's tools, you don't have to know Greek and Hebrew to do a good word study. All you need is a concordance, a Bible dictionary, and various Bible commentaries. Desktop study software or access to internet tools will simplify this process.

Cultural studies. There is an abundance of books available describing the ancient cultures that coexisted at the time original Bible texts were written. These resources will help you understand the nuances of the religious, geopolitical, familial, and anthropological realities of the ancient world. The study of ancient culture can be very enlightening and beneficial, helping you understand and interpret biblical texts.

Character studies. The Bible is filled with characters, literally and figuratively. The Bible is true and the people that inhabit its pages were real people with real problems, just like us. The Bible does not shy away from presenting both the strengths and weaknesses of those it portrays. This makes the characters in the Bible practical in the sense that we can relate to them and educational in the sense that we can learn from their successes and failures. There are volumes of books written about Bible characters and the ancient authors that wrote them.

Geographical studies. Biblical geography is the study of Bible lands and an examination of the places and geological features that are within the boundaries of those lands. Becoming familiar with the geographical background of the ancient biblical world is essential for a better understanding of the Bible. Modern maps, with overlays of ancient maps, provide valuable perspective as you read about specific rivers, mountains, details about topography, and even nations and empires that all had geographical boundaries.

Archeological studies. Christian archaeology is the science of studying ancient cultures that have impacted Christianity and Judaism and the Jewish and Christian cultures themselves. Not only are Christian archaeologists trying to discover new things about the past, they are trying to validate what we already know about the past and advance our understanding of the manners and customs of the peoples of the Bible. Modern excavations of ancient garbage dumps and abandoned cities have provided bits and pieces that give us clues to the past. The goal of Christian archaeology is to verify the essential truths of the Old and New Testaments through the physical artifacts of ancient peoples.

Early church studies. Studying the writings of Church Fathers is a branch of theology called Patristic studies. Scholars have produced volumes of materials documenting the theological and scriptural insights of our Church Fathers, such as Clement, Ignatius, and Polycarp. Developing an understanding of early church thought and the history of how Christian doctrine was developed will give you a sense of continuity with the community of saints worldwide and throughout the ages.

A word of caution about online searches. The Information Age ushered in a knowledge explosion and with the internet, we can get information easier than most of us would have imagined. However, just because it is online, doesn't mean that it is accurate. There were false teachers in the time of Paul the Apostle and there is false teaching today. Just because the site you see listed is ranked high doesn't mean that it is teaching solid doctrine. Check with your pastor or a trusted Christian friend who knows the Bible and ask them for help in finding materials that will guide you to accurate interpretation of the scriptures.

We love God's Word by reading it and studying it. Finally, we love God's Word by applying it to the way we live.

I love God's Word by applying it to the way I live.

Jesus had a problem with those that knew the Bible but were not living out what it says. He once told a crowd of people: "The teachers of religious law and the Pharisees are the official interpreters of the law of Moses. So, practice and obey whatever they tell you, but don't follow their example. For they don't practice what they teach" (Matthew 23:1-3).

We can read the Bible and even study it, but if we do not apply it to the way we live what good is it? Several biblical authors comment on this very issue.

> "But don't just listen to God's word. You must do what it says. Otherwise, you are only fooling yourselves" (James 1:22).

> "I have hidden your word in my heart, that I might not sin against you" (Psalms 119:11).

> "Let the word of Christ dwell in you richly, teaching and admonishing one another in all wisdom, singing psalms and hymns and spiritual songs, with thankfulness in your hearts to God" (Colossians 3:16, *ESV*).

As we read the Bible, we should study it for its true meaning, treasure it in our hearts, and then make sure we apply it to the way we live. We can let God's Word be part of our thinking and, together as a church, we can encourage each other to live what the Bible teaches. We will study more about living what the scriptures teach in the last two chapters, "Led by the Holy Spirit," and "Outwardly Focused."

INDIVIDUAL EXERCISE
A Healthy Christian Loves God's Word

PART 1: SELF-ASSESSMENT

Read each statement below and rate yourself according to the frequency in which that statement is true about you. Be honest with yourself. This is not a pass/fail quiz; it is simply a measuring tool to see where you are in your Christian walk as it relates to **loving God's Word**. Don't be afraid to admit that there are some areas where you need to improve. Admitting and committing to change is the way we become and stay spiritually healthy.

I read the Bible.

☐ regularly ☐ often ☐ sometimes ☐ no

I participate in a Bible study.

☐ regularly ☐ often ☐ sometimes ☐ no

I listen to Christian preachers and teachers on the radio, TV, or internet.

☐ regularly ☐ often ☐ sometimes ☐ no

I read Christian literature.

☐ regularly ☐ often ☐ sometimes ☐ no

I memorize Bible verses and try to understand its true meaning.

☐ regularly ☐ often ☐ sometimes ☐ no

PART 2: HEALTHY CHRISTIAN ACTION PLAN

After you complete the self-assessment, pray and ask God about areas you need to work on. Read the following commitment statement and identify personal goals that will help you achieve **loving God's Word** more. Record your goals and monitor your progress as you work toward achieving them. Consider sharing your goals with someone who will support you in your *Healthy Christian* action plan.

Commitment

I commit myself to improving my Christian health by taking the following action steps: I commit myself to improving my Christian health by taking the following action steps:

_____

_____

_____

_____

Bible Verse Resources

Review the Bible resource section in the back of this book. Select two verses that speak to you about **loving Jesus**. Let God speak to you through His Word. Enjoy being with Him. Listen to the truth God wants you to know through these verses. Sense Him speaking to you through them. Claim this biblical truth about you!

1. _____

2. _____

GROUP EXERCISE
A Healthy Christian Loves God's Word

Please review the following questions before you meet for group discussion or move on to the next lesson.

DISCUSSION 1

According to the verses below, what are the benefits of reading God's Word?

- "All scripture is inspired by God and is useful to teach us what is true and to make us realize what is wrong in our lives. It corrects us when we are wrong and teaches us to do what is right. God uses it to prepare and equip his people to do every good work" (2 Timothy 3:16-17).
- "People do not live by bread alone; rather, we live by every word that comes from the mouth of the Lord" (Deuteronomy 8:3).
- "Your word is a lamp to guide my feet and a light for my path" (Psalms 119:105).
- "The instructions of the Lord are perfect, reviving the soul. The decrees of the Lord are trustworthy, making wise the simple. The commandments of the Lord are right, bringing joy to the heart. The commands of the Lord are clear, giving insight for living" (Psalm 19:7-8).
- "And the scriptures give us hope and encouragement as we wait patiently for God's promises to be fulfilled" (Romans 15:4).
- "Let the message about Christ, in all its richness, fill your lives. Teach and counsel each other with all the wisdom he gives" (Colossians 3:16).
- "For the Word of God is living and powerful and sharper than any two-edged sword, piercing even to the dividing asunder of soul and spirit, and of the joints and marrow, and is a discerner of the thoughts and intents of the heart" (Hebrews 4:12).

Benefits: _____
_____
_____
_____
_____
_____
_____
_____

DISCUSSION 2

In this lesson, we reviewed Bible reading statistics provided by Ed Stetzer, LifeWay Research. Stetzer commented, "You can follow Christ and see Christianity as your source of truth, but if that truth does not permeate your thoughts, aspirations, and actions, you are not fully engaging the truth. God's Word is truth, so it should come as no surprise that reading and studying the Bible are still the activities that have the most impact on growth in this attribute of spiritual maturity. As basic as that is, there are still numerous churchgoers who are not reading the Bible regularly. You simply won't grow if you don't know God and spend time in God's Word."

What do you think about Stetzer's observations? _____

_____

_____

_____

_____

_____

_____

In what way do you feel Bible reading is crucial to developing a spiritual lifestyle? _____

_____

_____

_____

_____

_____

_____

DISCUSSION 3

How is reading the Bible different than reading a novel or non-fiction book? _____

_____

_____

_____

_____

_____

_____

DISCUSSION 4

What attitude should you have when sitting down to read God's Word? _____

_____

_____

_____

_____

_____

DISCUSSION 5

Paul wrote to Timothy: "Be a good worker, one who does not need to be ashamed and who correctly explains the word of truth" (2 Timothy 2:15).

What is the difference between reading the Bible and studying it? _____

_____

_____

_____

_____

_____

_____

_____

What Bible study aids can you use? _____

_____

_____

_____

_____

_____

_____

_____

_____

DISCUSSION 6

"The teachers of religious law and the Pharisees are the official interpreters of the law of Moses. So, practice and obey whatever they tell you, but don't follow their example. For they don't practice what they teach" (Matthew 23:1-3).

What bothered Jesus so much about the Pharisees? Can you think of an example of their hypocrisy?

_____

_____

_____

_____

_____

_____

_____

_____

_____

_____

_____

DISCUSSION 7

"But don't just listen to God's word. You must do what it says. Otherwise, you are only fooling yourselves" (James 1:22).

What did James mean in this passage? _____

_____

_____

_____

_____

_____

_____

_____

_____

What areas of life can we apply what James was saying? _____

_____

_____

_____

_____

_____

_____

_____

_____

_____

_____

DISCUSSION 8

Share one of the verses you selected from the Bible Verse Resources section that spoke to you about **loving God's Word**. How is this verse meaningful to you? _____

_____

_____

_____

_____

_____

_____

_____

_____

_____

_____

3

A Healthy Christian
is Emotionally Resilient

I am emotionally resilient
with the Fruit of the Spirit, through
a healing community, and by
relearning the truth.

A HEALTHY CHRISTIAN
IS EMOTIONALLY RESILIENT

The human infant is one of the most vulnerable of all creatures with tremendous needs that must be taken care of. A baby cannot see, feed itself, or move around on its own. It can't think or seeks its own protection. A baby can only cry, alerting others that they need assistance. Physically, the baby must be fed, cleaned up after, and protected from all danger. However, as a human grows older, they are able to take care of many of these needs themselves. Of course, not all of our needs are physical. We also have *soul needs*—emotional and spiritual needs that are important to our self-image and its survival. When our soul needs are unmet, they become *soul yearnings:*

- **Safety.** To be safe and comforted.
- **Purpose.** To have a personal purpose.
- **Belonging.** To know that you belong.
- **Significance.** To be significant and have honor.
- **Love.** To be loved and known as lovable.

When these soul needs are not fulfilled, they cause emotional conflict. They leave strongholds of doubt, fear, and longings that lurk in our hearts. We find ourselves believing lies about ourselves and trying various ways of escaping the emotional pain they create. For this, we need *emotional resilience*—the ability to bounce back from emotional pain.

We are full of emotions. We can't get away from them. However, the goal is not to avoid emotions, it is to regulate them. A Christian can do this by letting God, in His power, grace, and love, return us to deep joy and peace. This is what emotional resilience is all about. Resilience is the ability to bounce back from emotional pain and is beautifully portrayed in the verses of Psalm 42. Throughout the psalm, the author shares deep emotional angst. But each time, the psalmist ends up turning to God. We see this throughout the psalm.

- The psalmist cries out, "Why am I discouraged? Why is my heart so sad?" He later responds, "But I will put my hope in God!"
- The psalmist confesses, "Now I am deeply discouraged!" He later responds, "But I will remember You!"

The general position taken by the psalmist can be summed up with this verse: "Each day the Lord pours his unfailing love upon me, and through each night I sing his songs, praying to God who gives me life" (Psalm 42:8). Life has its emotional challenges, but we must not stop there. We have a choice. We can give our hearts to God, talk to Him, share our stories with Him, and let His love, concern, and

41

opinion of us, return us to joy. God desires us to be resilient and has given us three ways that we can do this:

1. By the Fruit of the Spirit
2. Through a healing community
3. By knowing the truth about who we are in Christ

I am emotionally resilient with the Fruit of the Spirit.

Emotional resilience is the ability to return to a positive emotional state of mind from emotional pain. For several years, I taught that we should return to peace and joy. It made sense and people responded well to the teaching. We have a choice and we can choose to trust God and return to a state of peace and joy.

"The Holy Spirit produces this kind of fruit in our lives: love, joy, peace, patience, kindness, goodness, faithfulness, gentleness, and self-control" (Galatians 5:22-23). One day, as I read these verses in Galatians 5, I realized that God offers us more than peace and joy. He offers us the Fruit of the Spirit. Talk about resilience! The Fruit of the Spirit covers all kinds of emotional pain in many types of situations.

- **Angry?** Return to love, gentleness, or self-control.
- **Worried?** Return to patience, peace, or joy.
- **Wounded?** Return to love, goodness, or joy.
- **Betrayed?** Return to faithfulness, peace, or love.

The fruit that the Holy Spirit produces in our lives results in us becoming more mature and our ability to be resilient when difficulties come our way. Jesus talked about the purpose of the Holy Spirit:

> "I will ask the Father and he will give you another Advocate, who will never leave you. He is the Holy Spirit, who leads into all truth. But when the Father sends the Advocate as my representative—that is, the Holy Spirit—he will teach you everything and will remind you of everything I have told you. I am leaving you with a gift— peace of mind and heart. And the peace I give is a gift the world cannot give. So, don't be troubled or afraid" (John 14: 16-17, 26-27).

Note that in two places, Jesus refers to the Holy Spirit as an *advocate*. He does, indeed, advocate on our behalf. But it is much more than that. In the original Greek, the word used here is *paraclete* which also means, comforter, encourager, or counselor. The Holy Spirit produces fruit in our lives and He is able to comfort, encourage, and counsel us. The Holy Spirit helps us mature and become resilient. The

Apostle Paul was a zealous missionary for Jesus. He faced persecution from the Jews, who saw him as a traitor and heretic, and the Gentiles who rebelled against Christianity as a religion. In the midst of conflict, when it would have been easy for Paul to give up, he wrote:

> "We are pressed on every side by troubles, but we are not crushed. We are perplexed, but not driven to despair. We are hunted down but never abandoned by God. That is why we never give up. Though our bodies are dying, our spirits are being renewed every day" (2 Corinthians 4:8-9, 16).

This is a perfect example of how the Holy Spirit comes to our aid by producing the Fruit of the Spirit in our lives. The Holy Spirit renews our spirits. This is more than simply refreshing us—it is about changing our state of mind. We are being renewed by the Holy Spirit through the presence of His fruit.

HOW WE RECEIVE THE FRUIT OF THE SPIRIT

The Holy Spirit is given to us at conversion. The Fruit of the Spirit is the byproduct of the relationship we have with the Holy Spirit. This is the kind of relationship where we spend time with Him, become keenly aware of His presence, and are in a constant communion with Him.

When we allow the Holy Spirit to rule in our hearts and choose out of love and obedience to do what He desires, we will see Him develop the fruit in our life. This won't be easy, however. We will be tempted to live according to our own desires. Paul suggests that we see these desires for what they are—wrong, selfish, sinful behaviors that we often do to escape from our painful emotions, thoughts, and predictions. When we see them as selfish acts to compensate for lies we believe about ourselves (no good, damaged goods, must look good for others, etc.), we can die to them (Paul said to nail them to the cross) and allow the Holy Spirit to give us the truth that comes from spiritual wisdom and understanding.

When we learn the truth of who we are in Christ and how much He really loves us, we can be joyful and thankful. Emotional resilience comes when we choose to return from painful emotions to the Fruit of the Spirit which is love, joy, peace, patience, kindness, goodness, faithfulness, gentleness, and self-control.

LOVE	JOY	PEACE
Return to love from…	*Return to joy from…*	*Return to peace from…*
• Dislike	• Depression	• Disagreement
• Hatefulness	• Misery	• Distress
• Apathy	• Sadness	• Fighting
• Treachery	• Sorrow	• Frustration
• Selfishness	• Unhappiness	• Worry
• Thoughtlessness	• Mourning	• Fear

PATIENCE	KINDNESS	GOODNESS
Return to patience from…	*Return to kindness from…*	*Return to goodness from…*
▪ Indifference	▪ Resentment	▪ Corruption
▪ Resistance	▪ Hostility	▪ Cruelty
▪ Arousal	▪ Ill-will	▪ Dishonor
▪ Agitation	▪ Indifference	▪ Evil
▪ Intolerance	▪ Meanness	▪ Indecency
▪ Defiance	▪ Mercilessness	▪ Wickedness

FAITHFULNESS	GENTLENESS	SELF-CONTROL
Return to faithfulness from…	*Return to gentleness from…*	*Return to self-control from…*
▪ Disloyalty	▪ Anger	▪ Instability
▪ Treachery	▪ Frustration	▪ Agitation
▪ Disregard	▪ Hardness	▪ Panic
▪ Inconstancy	▪ Revenge	▪ Lust
▪ Dishonesty	▪ Hurt	▪ Temptation
▪ Falseness	▪ Roughness	▪ Relapse

I am emotionally resilient through a healing community.

We were created as relational beings. God originally created us to have fellowship with Him. He also said that it was not good for man to live alone, indicating our innate need for relationships. Take another look at our *soul yearnings*.

- **Safety.** To be safe and comforted.
- **Purpose.** To have a personal purpose.
- **Belonging.** To know that you belong.
- **Significance.** To be significant and have honor.
- **Love.** To be loved and known as lovable.

All of these were meant to be lived out in a loving caring community. The early church was a healing community. Look at Acts 2 where it talks about the church in its infancy. Persecution, pagan religions, poverty, slavery, and Roman occupation; and the church was born in very unstable conditions. However, through obedience to God, their commitment to having a loving and caring fellowship sustained them and caused the church to grow.

> "All the believers devoted themselves to the apostles' teaching, and to fellowship, and to sharing in meals, and to prayer. A deep sense of awe came over them all, and the apostles performed many miraculous signs and wonders. And all the believers met together in one place and shared everything they had. They sold their property and possessions and shared the money with those in need. They worshiped together at the

Temple each day, met in homes for the Lord's Supper, and shared their meals with great joy and generosity—all the while praising God and enjoying the goodwill of all the people. And each day the Lord added to their fellowship those who were being saved" (Acts 2:42-47).

Why would they love each other and care for each other? Because they were brothers and sisters in Christ. Paul tells us that we are all adopted into the same family, sharing the love of the same Heavenly Father. In Romans, Paul writes:

"You have not received a spirit that makes you fearful slaves. Instead, you received God's Spirit when he adopted you as his own children. Now we call him, 'Abba, Father.' For his Spirit joins with our spirit to affirm that we are God's children" (Romans 8:15-16).

We become emotionally resilient when we are with people that are happy to be with us, share unconditional love for us, and affirm who we are as fellow believers in Christ. This is how our churches should be. God is our Father and we are siblings called to love one another. Paul writes to the church in Ephesus about the kind of fellowship they should have—the kind of community with each other that breeds resilience:

"Lead a life worthy of your calling, for you have been called by God. Always be humble and gentle. Be patient with each other, making allowance for each other's faults because of your love. Make every effort to keep yourselves united in the Spirit, binding yourselves together with peace" (Ephesians 4:1-3).

The author of Hebrews also encourages us to fellowship with each other in love: "Let us think of ways to motivate one another to acts of love and good works. And let us not neglect our meeting together, as some people do, but encourage one another" (Hebrews 10:24-25).

The author of Hebrews paints a picture of a model community of acceptance and attachment. A person can be themselves and get the help in areas where they need to mature. It is impossible to get to know everyone in a church; the larger the church, the more difficult it is to have intimate fellowship. However, there is nothing stopping you from building community with a smaller group. There are many ways to be part of a healing community within the larger church.

BE PART OF A HEALING COMMUNITY IN SMALL GROUPS

Bible Study Groups. Bible studies help you grow in Bible knowledge and provide you with the opportunity to get to know other believers and develop lasting friendships.

Common Interest Groups. There are many interests, activities, and hobbies that people have an affinity for and can enjoy together. Common interest groups from your church promote spiritual and emotional growth as you pursue mutual interests together.

Support and Recovery Groups. A loving and caring support group is an excellent way to heal from painful experiences and emotions. Whether it is grief, addiction, emotional issues, parenting, or family relationships, a support group can offer the kind of growth opportunities you need.

Service Ministry Teams. Ministry teams, such as children's ministry, choir, feeding the homeless, ushering, sports, and leadership teams, are great opportunities to be part of a close-knit fellowship that nurtures and cares for each other.

A healing community is just that—a community in which its members can be healed emotionally. This happens when we come with our humanness exposed, admit our needs, and help each other in love. There are *no perfect people* and each of us must do our part to strive for a Christian fellowship that is accepting, loving, and living for Christ. We don't need to put on masks. We can come as we are and mature as we grow in the Lord through a loving community.

> "Don't think you are better than you really are. Be honest in your evaluation of yourselves, measuring yourselves by the faith God has given us. Just as our bodies have many parts and each part has a special function, so it is with Christ's body. We are many parts of one body, and we all belong to each other. Don't just pretend to love others. Really love them. Hate what is wrong. Hold tightly to what is good. Love each other with genuine affection and take delight in honoring each other. Never be lazy but work hard and serve the Lord enthusiastically. Rejoice in our confident hope. Be patient in trouble and keep on praying. When God's people are in need, be ready to help them. Always be eager to practice hospitality. Bless those who persecute you. Don't curse them; pray that God will bless them. Be happy with those who are happy, and weep with those who weep. Live in harmony with each other. Don't be too proud to enjoy the company of ordinary people. And don't think you know it all!" (Romans 12:3-5, 9-16).

> "I appeal to you, dear brothers and sisters, by the authority of our Lord Jesus Christ, to live in harmony with each other. Let there be no divisions in the church. Rather, be of one mind, united in thought and purpose" (1 Corinthians 1:10).

> "Finally, all of you should be of one mind. Sympathize with each other. Love each other as brothers and sisters. Be tenderhearted and keep a humble attitude" (1 Peter 3:8).

"So, put to death the sinful, earthly things lurking within you. Have nothing to do with sexual immorality, impurity, lust, and evil desires. Don't be greedy, for a greedy person is an idolater, worshiping the things of this world. Because of these sins, the anger of God is coming. You used to do these things when your life was still part of this world. But now is the time to get rid of anger, rage, malicious behavior, slander, and dirty language. Don't lie to each other, for you have stripped off your old sinful nature and all its wicked deeds. Put on your new nature and be renewed as you learn to know your Creator and become like him" (Colossians 3:5-10).

We will mature in Christ as we fellowship with other believers that are committed to accepting and loving one another.

I am emotionally resilient by relearning the truth.

The third way to become emotionally resilient is to know the truth about ourselves. One of the key principles of emotional resilience is what I have called *Emotional Relearning*™. As I studied, taught, and wrote about emotional resilience, it soon became apparent that I was dealing with *learned* behavior. The standard approaches to emotional healing have been cognitive in nature.

For years, we have taught that when a person has a wrong notion about themselves they just need to know what is true to correct their thinking. This works in many cases. But as I studied, experimented with my own thinking, and counseled others, I found that there was a different kind of learning—a type of learning that many of the people I was working with experienced. It was learning that came from *trauma*, reinforced emotionally and tied into the amygdala-based alarm system.

The amygdala is the part of the brain's limbic or emotional center and acts like a guard shack to protect us. If it perceives danger, because of the previous trauma-based learning, it highjacks the brain and puts it into the fight/flight/freeze mode. Unlike logical left brain learning, trauma-based learning is right brain learning. Left brain logic alone does not solve the problem. It is like trying to convince a beautiful person who thinks they are ugly that they are beautiful—they just won't buy it. They have somehow *emotionally* learned that they are ugly and, even though it is a lie, it is deeply and emotionally believed. A lie about oneself that was emotionally learned can be changed when the truth is emotionally *relearned*.

Emotional Relearning™ is the practice of correcting a lie about ourselves by learning the truth emotionally. The lie was emotionally learned and feels true—not due to the logic of the belief but due to the enormous emotion carried with it. The way we counter that wrong belief is to have a source of truth that is credible enough to believe and powerful enough to overcome the source of the lie. When a credible source corrects the awful lie that we believe about ourselves and authoritatively shares the truth with us, it is a moving experience. It is liberating. It is exhilarating. This is what God can do for us! He is the final authority and what He believes about you trumps all the lies that were introduced and/or reinforced by others.

HOW EMOTIONAL RELEARNING™ WORKS

Name what you are feeling. The first step is to stop when you are sensing that you are over-emoting. Name the emotion you are feeling. This also works after the fact by going back to the time you were over emotional. Name the emotion.

Identify what you are believing about yourself. When you sense emotions and feelings, ask yourself what you're believing about yourself at that very moment. What you believe may elicit strong emotions, but it doesn't necessarily mean it is true.

- Believing that you are "worthless garbage" is emotional, but not true.
- Believing that your mother did not love you is emotional and may, to some extent, be true. It happens.

However true or false, what we believe has a perceived consequence.

Define the perceived consequence of your self-belief. When you have a self-belief that is negative, there is usually a perceived consequence that you are believing as well. Take the example of believing you are a worthless piece of garbage. What do you usually do with garbage? You throw it away. How do you think that would affect a child that doesn't know any better? They would be terrified by the deep-down belief that as garbage, they, too, could be thrown away or abandoned. When an emotional and spiritual need that is important to our self-image and its survival (soul need) is threatened, it elicits primal fear in the form of an intense "I'm going to die" type of reaction. We don't actually die, of course. But because the lie was believed *emotionally*, this child will grow up with the belief that there is something wrong with them. And when they get into a situation where that belief is highlighted, they will go into *fight* or *flight* mode. The secret to overcoming this is to change our beliefs.

Examine what you are believing. Calm yourself down and begin to examine what you are believing. Be your own observer—a detective with an objective view. Make sure you have a grasp on the belief that is bothering you. Remember it is only a thought. It will not hurt you. In fact, most of our negative beliefs that bother us are rooted in lies.

Invite God to share the truth with you. This part is deeply spiritual. God loves you and knows the truth about you. Invite Him to share the truth with you. Let's return to the example of the low self-image, believing that you are no good, broken goods, and worthless. As you sense that belief, come to God and ask:

"Lord Jesus, I feel like I am no good; that I'm a broken piece of garbage. What do you believe about me? Is there anything You want to tell me?"

This is not the time to rush. Focus, wait and let God speak to your heart. He could do this through a verse that comes to your mind, a feeling, an image, a phrase, or a bodily experience. It may simply be an assurance that what you are believing is not true. Everyone is different. God meets us where we are individually and in a way that will speak to our hearts. God will share the truth with you.

You may not feel as though you received a specific response from God or you're not sure. Don't dismay! Remember that many of these lies have been believed thousands of times and have become strongholds in your heart and mind. Also, you may not have much experience listening to God. Many of us are used to praying to God but may not have much experience in listening to Him or hearing Him. Don't give up—continue in His presence.

Bible verses are provided in the back of this book in The Bible Resources section: Biblical Truth About You. Verses are grouped into two categories: 1) standard Bible translation verses for your meditation and 2) Bible verses that have been paraphrased, rewritten into the first person, for personal affirmation. Meditate on these scriptures and let God speak to you through His Word. Enjoy being with Him. Listen to the truth God wants you to know through these verses. Sense Him sharing them with you.

Consider the truth and listen for disbelief. If you receive some truth, stop and think about it. Try saying it out loud. When you do, watch for a fearful response, disbelief, or a sense of rejection. Why? Because it is hard to stop believing something you've believed for a long time, even if it's not true. Remember the beautiful person who thinks they are ugly that we mentioned earlier? They are not going to give up that belief without a fight. Likewise, the lies you believe about yourself are strongholds coming from wounds that are emotionally believed. That means that they cause an emotional reaction rather than logical reasoning.

A phobia is a good example. Try telling someone that it is safe to go on an elevator when they have a phobic fear of it. Their emotions will argue with you. Likewise, when you are trying to contradict a long-standing negative belief about yourself, you will get pushback. This is good! You may be asking, "How can that be good?" It is good because you have gone from an autonomic kneejerk reaction to the negative belief to a place where you are considering an alternative belief. This is the first step toward creating a new healthy concept of yourself.

Renounce the lies and pronounce the truth. The next step is to renounce the lie and pronounce the new truth. If you still have nagging doubts, realize that it is not intellectual but emotional and that it is coming from *faulty wiring*.

It is no different than a smoke detector going off when there is no smoke or fire. How long would you put up with that? By the time you unplugged the battery from a blaring smoke alarm for the fifth time in the same day, no doubt you would simply and easily throw it out. It is the same thing here. You are believing lies about yourself that are sending you emotional signals but they're nothing more than false alarms. They are lies. It feels like the truth, but it isn't.

You need to replace the lie with the truth. Here are some lie versus truth examples:

LIE:	*I am worthless and have no significance.*
TRUTH:	*I am God's child.*
PROOF:	"But to all who believed him and accepted him, he gave the right to become children of God" (John 1:12).

LIE:	*It's too late; I cannot change.*
TRUTH:	*I am a new creation in Christ.*
PROOF:	"Let the Spirit renew your thoughts and attitudes. Put on your new nature, created to be like God—truly righteous and holy" (Ephesians 4:23-24).

LIE:	*I am bad, unforgivable, and rejected by God and man.*
TRUTH:	*I am forgiven and accepted by God because of Christ Jesus.*
PROOF:	"There is no condemnation for those who belong to Christ Jesus. And because you belong to him, the power of the life-giving Spirit has freed you from the power of sin that leads to death" (Romans 8:1-2).

LIE:	*I am unlovable and unwanted.*
TRUTH:	*I am deeply loved by Jesus.*
PROOF:	[Jesus speaking] "I have loved you even as the Father has loved me. Remain in my love" (John 15:9).

LIE:	*I am nobody; I have no significance.*
TRUTH:	*I am born again, entitled to great spiritual blessings because of God's love for me.*
PROOF:	"All praise to God, the Father of our Lord Jesus Christ, who has blessed us with every spiritual blessing in the heavenly realms because we are united with Christ" (Ephesians 1:3).

> **LIE:** *My life is meaningless, and I have no purpose.*
>
> **TRUTH:** *I am God's ambassador, created to do His will on earth by doing good.*
>
> **PROOF:** "God saved you by his grace when you believed. And you can't take credit for this; it is a gift from God. Salvation is not a reward for the good things we have done, so none of us can boast about it. For we are God's masterpiece. He has created us anew in Christ Jesus, so we can do the good things he planned for us long ago" (Ephesians 2:8-10).

Affirm the new truth. You received a new truth about yourself. If it came from God, you know you can trust it. Now it is a matter of reinforcing it emotionally and logically again and again until it becomes second-nature. This is when we use Bible verses, prayer, and meditation. God's truth is transformational and can break the bondage of previous negative emotional learning and create powerful truth through emotional and spiritual *relearning*. God wants you to be transformed by Him and His Word. Don't be afraid to admit that there are some areas where you need to improve. Admitting and committing to change is the way we become and stay spiritually healthy.

"Don't copy the behavior and customs of this world, but let God transform you into a new person by changing the way you think" (Romans 12:2).

"Fix your thoughts on what is true, and honorable, and right, and pure, and lovely, and admirable. Think about things that are excellent and worthy of praise" (Philippians 4:8).

"We use God's mighty weapons, not worldly weapons, to knock down the strongholds of human reasoning and to destroy false arguments. We destroy every proud obstacle that keeps people from knowing God. We capture their rebellious thoughts and teach them to obey Christ" (2 Corinthians 10:4-5).

"Anyone who belongs to Christ has become a new person. The old life is gone; a new life has begun" (2 Corinthians 5:17).

"Throw off your old sinful nature and your former way of life, which is corrupted by lust and deception. Instead, let the Spirit renew your thoughts and attitudes. Put on your new nature, created to be like God—truly righteous and holy" (Ephesians 4:22-24).

"Put on your new nature and be renewed as you learn to know your Creator and become like him" (Colossians 3:10).

Note: Go to "Believing What God Believes About Me—the Bible Verse Resource section in the back of the book—for more scriptures that will help you with emotional resilience.

OTHER WAYS TO EMOTIONALLY RELEARN AND BECOME RESILIENT

Counseling. You can increase your emotional resilience through a good counseling relationship. A professional counselor can help you gain insight and give you the healthy attachment you need to mature.

Support groups. Support groups can help you zero in on the issues that you are struggling with and can help you develop more emotional resilience by challenging you to grow as a person in a safe, supporting group environment.

INDIVIDUAL EXERCISE
A Healthy Christian is Emotionally Resilient

PART 1: SELF-ASSESSMENT

Read each statement below and rate yourself according to the frequency in which that statement is true about you. Be honest with yourself. This is not a pass/fail quiz; it is simply a measuring tool to see where you are in your Christian walk as it relates to being **emotionally resilient**. Don't be afraid to admit that there are some areas where you need to improve. Admitting and committing to change is the way we become and stay spiritually healthy.

I correct my negative thinking with the truth.

☐ regularly ☐ often ☐ sometimes ☐ no

I know when I become emotionally upset; I stop, relax, and work through it.

☐ regularly ☐ often ☐ sometimes ☐ no

I return to peace and joy from painful emotions.

☐ regularly ☐ often ☐ sometimes ☐ no

I have someone I share my inner thoughts with and they support me.

☐ regularly ☐ often ☐ sometimes ☐ no

I lean on God and His Word for comfort and strength.

☐ regularly ☐ often ☐ sometimes ☐ no

I seek professional help when I become too overwhelmed.

☐ regularly ☐ often ☐ sometimes ☐ no

I keep a clear conscience, free from bitterness, unconfessed sin, and unforgiveness.

☐ regularly ☐ often ☐ sometimes ☐ no

I am living with the various Fruit of the Spirit evident in my life.

Love...............	☐ regularly	☐ often	☐ sometimes	☐ no
Joy..................	☐ regularly	☐ often	☐ sometimes	☐ no
Peace..............	☐ regularly	☐ often	☐ sometimes	☐ no
Patience.............	☐ regularly	☐ often	☐ sometimes	☐ no
Kindness...........	☐ regularly	☐ often	☐ sometimes	☐ no
Goodness...........	☐ regularly	☐ often	☐ sometimes	☐ no
Faithfulness........	☐ regularly	☐ often	☐ sometimes	☐ no
Gentleness.........	☐ regularly	☐ often	☐ sometimes	☐ no
Self-control.........	☐ regularly	☐ often	☐ sometimes	☐ no

I am involved in a small group on a regular basis.

☐ regularly ☐ often ☐ sometimes ☐ no

I have a close circle of Christian friends; we pray, support and care for each other.

☐ regularly ☐ often ☐ sometimes ☐ no

I belong to a ministry in which I have close friends.

☐ regularly ☐ often ☐ sometimes ☐ no

PART 2: HEALTHY CHRISTIAN ACTION PLAN

After you complete the self-assessment, pray and ask God about areas you need to work on. Read the following commitment statement and identify personal goals that will help you achieve being more **emotionally resilient**. Record your goals and monitor your progress as you work toward achieving them. Consider sharing your goals with someone who will support you in your *Healthy Christian* action plan.

Commitment

I commit myself to improving my Christian health by taking the following action steps: I commit myself to improving my Christian health by taking the following action steps:

_____
_____
_____
_____
_____
_____
_____
_____

Bible Verse Resources

Review the Bible resource section in the back of this book. Select two verses that speak to you about being **emotionally resilient**. Let God speak to you through His Word. Enjoy being with Him. Listen to the truth God wants you to know through these verses. Sense Him speaking to you through them. Claim this biblical truth about you!

1. _____
2. _____

GROUP EXERCISE
A Healthy Christian is Emotionally Resilient

Please review the following questions before you meet for group discussion or move on to the next lesson.

DISCUSSION 1

Unmet emotional and spiritual needs that are important to our self-image and its survival become *soul yearnings:*

- **Safety.** To be safe and comforted.
- **Purpose.** To have a personal purpose.
- **Belonging.** To know that you belong.
- **Significance.** To be significant and have honor.
- **Love.** To be loved and known as lovable.

How can knowing God satisfy these soul yearnings? _____

_____

_____

_____

_____

_____

_____

_____

_____

_____

_____

DISCUSSION 2

In Galatians, Paul lists the Fruit of the Spirit: "The Holy Spirit produces this kind of fruit in our lives: love, joy, peace, patience, kindness, goodness, faithfulness, gentleness, and self-control" (Galatians 5:22-23). Which Fruit of the Spirit will help when you experience the following emotions?

- Anger _____
- Sadness _____
- Disgust _____
- Anxiety _____

DISCUSSION 3

"All the believers devoted themselves to the apostles' teaching, and to fellowship, and to sharing in meals, and to prayer. A deep sense of awe came over them all, and the apostles performed many miraculous signs and wonders. And all the believers met together in one place and shared everything they had. They sold their property and possessions and shared the money with those in need. They worshiped together at the Temple each day, met in homes for the Lord's Supper, and shared their meals with great joy and generosity—all the while praising God and enjoying the goodwill of all the people. And each day the Lord added to their fellowship those who were being saved" (Acts 2:42-47).

How realistic is this for the church today? _____

_____

_____

_____

_____

_____

What could you and your church do to be closer to this example? _____

_____

_____

_____

_____

_____

DISCUSSION 4

Churches need to be a healing community. They need to be safe, loving and nurturing.

Are churches a safe place? _____

_____

_____

_____

_____

_____

Do churches have cliques?_____

_____

_____

_____

_____

_____

How can divisions, cliques, or an unsafe environment be remedied? _____

_____

_____

_____

_____

_____

DISCUSSION 5

"Lead a life worthy of your calling, for you have been called by God. Always be humble and gentle. Be patient with each other, making allowance for each other's faults because of your love. Make every effort to keep yourselves united in the Spirit, binding yourselves together with peace" (Ephesians 4:1-3).

"I appeal to you, dear brothers and sisters, by the authority of our Lord Jesus Christ, to live in harmony with each other. Let there be no divisions in the church. Rather, be of one mind, united in thought and purpose" (1 Corinthians 1:10).

"Finally, all of you should be of one mind. Sympathize with each other. Love each other as brothers and sisters. Be tenderhearted and keep a humble attitude" (1 Peter 3:8).

How can obeying these verses help create a better fellowship at church? _____

_____

_____

_____

_____

_____

DISCUSSION 6

"Let us think of ways to motivate one another to acts of love and good works. And let us not neglect our meeting together, as some people do, but encourage one another" (Hebrews 10:24-25).

How can small groups assist people in getting to know each other better and help create a healing community? _____

_____

_____

_____

_____

_____

Many churches have Bible study groups. What kind of affinity or special interest groups, support groups, or ministry teams could your church start that would generate fellowship among your members? _____

_____

_____

_____

_____

_____

_____

_____

DISCUSSION 7

"Don't think you are better than you really are. Be honest in your evaluation of yourselves, measuring yourselves by the faith God has given us. Just as our bodies have many parts and each part has a special function, so it is with Christ's body. We are many parts of one body, and we all belong to each other. –Don't just pretend to love others. Really love them. Hate what is wrong. Hold tightly to what is good. Love each other with genuine affection and take delight in honoring each other. Never be lazy but work hard and serve the Lord enthusiastically. Rejoice in our confident hope. Be patient in trouble and keep on praying. When God's people are in need, be ready to help them. Always be eager to practice hospitality. Bless those who persecute you. Don't curse them; pray that God will bless them. Be happy with those who are happy, and weep with those who weep. Live in harmony with each other. Don't be too proud to enjoy the company of ordinary people. And don't think you know it all" (Romans 12:3-5, 9-16).

"I appeal to you, dear brothers and sisters, by the authority of our Lord Jesus Christ, to live in harmony with each other. Let there be no divisions in the church. Rather, be of one mind, united in thought and purpose" (Romans 1:10).

"Finally, all of you should be of one mind. Sympathize with each other. Love each other as brothers and sisters. Be tenderhearted and keep a humble attitude" (1 Peter 3:14).

"So, put to death the sinful, earthly things lurking within you. Have nothing to do with sexual immorality, impurity, lust, and evil desires. Don't be greedy, for a greedy person is an idolater, worshiping the things of this world. Because of these sins, the anger of God is coming. You used to do these things when your life was still part of this world. But now is the time to get rid of anger, rage, malicious behavior, slander, and dirty language. Don't lie to each other, for you have stripped off your old sinful nature and all its wicked deeds. Put on your new nature and be renewed as you learn to know your Creator and become like him" (Colossians 3:5-10).

What are some of the positive ways we are to treat each other in the church to become a nurturing and healing community? _____
_____
_____
_____
_____
_____
_____

What can a church do to become a nurturing and healing community? _____
_____
_____
_____
_____
_____
_____

DISCUSSION 8

We become emotionally resilient when we replace self-lies with the truth. Emotional resilience is the ability to bounce back from painful emotional episodes. One of the key ways to do this is to identify the lies we believe about ourselves and replace them with the truth. We do this by zeroing in on our feelings and asking ourselves four questions: What am I feeling? What am I believing about myself? What is the perceived consequence of that belief? What is the truth?

What negative things in the past have you believed about yourself? _____
_____
_____
_____
_____
_____

What do you think God would say is the truth about you? _____
_____
_____
_____
_____
_____
_____

59

When lies come against you, what can you do to combat them and find the truth? _____

_____

_____

_____

_____

_____

_____

DISCUSSION 9

Share one of the verses you selected from the Bible Verse Resources section that spoke to you about being emotionally resilient. How is this verse meaningful to you? _____

_____

_____

_____

_____

_____

_____

4

A Healthy Christian is Led by the Spirit

The Holy Spirit is God and lives inside me.
I listen to His guidance and teaching
and I'm led and controlled by Him.

A HEALTHY CHRISTIAN
IS LED BY THE SPIRIT

The next sign of a *Healthy Christian* is being led by the Holy Spirit. When it comes to equipping us for ministry, we have the most essential ingredient for a successful life imaginable. When we became born-again, we received the indwelling presence of the Holy Spirit into our very being. Imagine. God in His infinite wisdom created a way for each of us to be led personally by Him! This guidance is given through the Holy Spirit. Jesus attested to this fact: "It is good for you that I am going away. Unless I go away, the Counselor will not come to you; but if I go, I will send him to you" (John 16: 7).

Being led by the Holy Spirit means that we need to do three things: 1) acknowledge that He is God and lives inside us, 2) listen to His guidance and teaching, and 3) allow ourselves to be led and controlled by Him.

The Holy Spirit is God and lives inside me.

It is beyond the scope of this workbook to go into a long treatise on who the Holy Spirit is, but we cannot talk about the Christian life without mentioning this important part of the Trinity.

THE HOLY SPIRIT IS GOD

Word pictures help us to better understand concepts. Unfortunately, due to the influence of television and movies, we're tempted to think of the Holy Spirit as some ghost-like entity that is totally separated from God Himself. The truth is, we believe in one God who has chosen to manifest Himself in triune form. We relate to God and His love as our Father, to the way God wants us to live, and to the forgiveness of our sins through His Son Jesus Christ. However, God also chooses to relate to us by becoming part of who we are through His Spirit. A helpful way of putting the Holy Spirit into perspective is to think of Him as our Holy *God's* Spirit. This is not an inferior, diluted part of God. It is God in spirit form living in us.

THE HOLY SPIRIT LIVES INSIDE CHRISTIANS

John tells us about the Holy Spirit living inside of us:

> "And I will ask the Father, and he will give you another Counselor to be with you forever—the Spirit of truth. The world cannot accept him, because it neither sees him nor knows him. But you know him, for he lives with you and will be in you" (John 14:16-18).

"Don't you know that you yourselves are God's temple and that God's Spirit lives in you?" (1 Corinthians 3:16).

"No one has ever seen God; but if we love one another, God lives in us and his love is made complete in us. We know that we live in him and he in us because he has given us of his Spirit" (1 John 4:12-13).

We are to have a relationship with the Holy Spirit. More than just living inside of us, Paul explains that we have a relationship with Him:

"May the grace of the Lord Jesus Christ, and the love of God, and the fellowship of the Holy Spirit be with you all" (2 Corinthians 13:14).

"And hope does not disappoint us, because God has poured out his love into our hearts by the Holy Spirit, whom he has given us" (Romans 5:5).

I listen to the Holy Spirit's guidance and teaching.

If we are going to be led by the Holy Spirit, then we need to learn to listen to Him. Jesus told us about the Holy Spirit: "And I will ask the Father, and he will give you another Counselor to be with you forever—the Spirit of truth" (John 14:16-17).

THE HOLY SPIRIT GUIDES US

One of the roles of the Holy Spirit in our lives is as our personal *Counselor*. Some translations use the word *Comforter*. The Holy Spirit gives us insight, wisdom, and peace—powerful allies in living our lives! Discouragement, misunderstandings, and temptations happen to each of us.

The beauty of the Holy Spirit is that He communes with us personally, in our inner being. He speaks truth to us. As the inward expression of God, the Holy Spirit encourages us and gives us peace, assurance, and hope: "But the Counselor, the Holy Spirit, whom the Father will send in my name, will teach you all things and will remind you of everything I have said to you" (John 14:26).

But do we listen? Paul shares how the Holy Spirit knows the thoughts of God and wants to communicate them to us:

"No eye has seen, no ear has heard, no mind has conceived what God has prepared for those who love him but God has revealed it to us by his Spirit. The Spirit searches all things, even the deep things of God. For who among men knows the thoughts of a man except the man's spirit within him? In the same way, no one knows the thoughts of God except the Spirit of God. We have not received the spirit of the world but the Spirit who is from God, that we may understand what God has freely given us. This is what we speak, not in words taught us by human wisdom but in words taught by the Spirit, expressing spiritual truths in spiritual words. The man without the Spirit does not accept the things that come from the Spirit of God, for they are foolishness to him, and he cannot understand them, because they are spiritually discerned. The spiritual man makes judgments about all things, but he himself is not subject to any man's judgment: For who has known the mind of the Lord that he may instruct him? But we have the mind of Christ" (1 Corinthians 2:9-16).

THE HOLY SPIRIT SPEAKS THROUGH GOD'S WORD

God wants to speak to us, teach us, and guide us through the Bible with the Holy Spirit as our personal teacher. The Apostle Paul wrote about the importance of using the Bible as a guide for our lives.

"All scripture is inspired by God and is useful to teach us what is true and to make us realize what is wrong in our lives. It corrects us when we are wrong and teaches us to do what is right. God uses it to prepare and equip his people to do every good work" (2 Timothy 3:16-17).

You can call upon the Holy Spirit to teach and guide you using the Bible.

I am led and controlled by the Holy Spirit.

Paul taught on being led by the Holy Spirit in various letters to the early church.

"Since we are living by the Spirit, let us follow the Spirit's leading in every part of our lives" (Galatians 5:25).

"Those who are dominated by the sinful nature think about sinful things, but those who are controlled by the Holy Spirit think about things that please the Spirit. So, letting your sinful nature control your mind leads to death. But letting the Spirit control your mind leads to life and peace" (Romans 8:5-6).

"But you are not controlled by your sinful nature. You are controlled by the Spirit if you have the Spirit of God living in you" (Romans 8:9).

"But the Holy Spirit produces this kind of fruit in our lives: love, joy, peace, patience, kindness, goodness, faithfulness, gentleness, and self-control. There is no law against these things! Those who belong to Christ Jesus have nailed the passions and desires of their sinful nature to his cross and crucified them there. Since we are living by the Spirit, let us follow the Spirit's leading in every part of our lives" (Galatians 5:22-25).

"Those who live according to the sinful nature have their minds set on what that nature desires, but those who live in accordance with the Spirit have their minds set on what the Spirit desires. The mind of sinful man is death, but the mind controlled by the Spirit is life and peace; the sinful mind is hostile to God. It does not submit to God's law, nor can it do so. Those controlled by the sinful nature cannot please God. You, however, are controlled not by the sinful nature but by the Spirit, if the Spirit of God lives in you. And if anyone does not have the Spirit of Christ, he does not belong to Christ" (Romans 8:5-9).

In Romans 8, Paul shares how the Holy Spirit is our source of Christian living. He says that we need to live in accordance to and under the control of the Spirit. Another way that Paul referred to a Spirit-led life was to describe it as being Spirit-*filled*. It is interesting to note that Jesus was filled with the Holy Spirit: "Jesus, full of the Holy Spirit, returned from the Jordan and was led by the Spirit in the desert" (Luke 4:1). If Jesus needed to be filled with the Holy Spirit and was led by the Holy Spirit, shouldn't we do likewise?

Paul explains what it means to be filled with the Spirit using a metaphor:

"So be careful how you live. Don't live like fools, but like those who are wise. Make the most of every opportunity in these evil days. Don't act thoughtlessly but understand what the Lord wants you to do. Don't be drunk with wine, because that will ruin your life. Instead, be filled with the Holy Spirit" (Ephesians 5:15-18).

There is only one way to get drunk. You get drunk by being filled with alcohol until the amount that you consume has you under its influence. This is not a description of casual drink in moderation—this is excessive drinking, so much so that you become drunk. Instead of becoming drunk with wine, Paul admonishes us to have the same *insatiable appetite* for the guidance and fellowship of the Holy Spirit. When we insatiably meditate on God's Word and pray—more than a casual occurrence of reading a few verses or a mealtime prayer—we will become under the influence of the Holy Spirit's leading in our daily lives. In the original language, the tense used for the word *filled* is not a one-time action. It means "to be filled and keep on being filled."

Going back to the metaphor, consuming an excessive amount of wine on a Friday does not keep you drunk until the following weekend. The effect of the wine soon dissipates. To continually remain drunk, you must continually drink wine. When we became born-again, we received the indwelling presence of the Holy Spirit. But to remain under His influence, to be Spirit-led, we must continually acknowledge His presence and listen to His teaching and guidance.

SPIRIT-LED IN OUR DAILY LIVING

Sin happens. There are no perfect people. We all have the flesh side of our nature that constantly tempts us. Paul talks about these to the Galatian church:

> "When you follow the desires of your sinful nature, the results are very clear: sexual immorality, impurity, lustful pleasures, idolatry, sorcery, hostility, quarreling, jealousy, outbursts of anger, selfish ambition, dissension, division, envy, drunkenness, wild parties, and other sins like these" (Galatians 5:19-21).

In the book of John, Jesus tells us: "When he [the Holy Spirit] comes, he will convict the world of its sin, and of God's righteousness, and of the coming judgment" (John 16:8).

The Holy Spirit convicts us of sin. At that point, we have a choice. Do we agree with God and admit that we have done wrong or do we ignore, justify or rationalize it? If we agree, then we confess it to God and ask for His forgiveness and repent. By repenting, we commit to a different course of action. We say no and act as if we are dead to it. Dead people do not sin. That is why Paul wrote: "Those who belong to Christ Jesus have nailed the passions and desires of their sinful nature to his cross and crucified them there" (Galatians 5:24).

Paul talks about this to the Ephesian church as well. In the following verse, he suggests that we *throw off* our sinful nature and *put on* Spirit-led behavior. It is this throwing off and putting on that allows the Holy Spirit to renew our thoughts and attitudes.

> "Since you have heard about Jesus and have learned the truth that comes from him, throw off your old sinful nature and your former way of life, which is corrupted by lust and deception. Instead, let the Spirit renew your thoughts and attitudes. Put on your new nature, created to be like God—truly righteous and holy" (Ephesians 4:21-24).

It is not just dying to our sin that will make the difference. We must also come alive to the Holy Spirit and let Him lead us in the better way to live. We throw off sin and put on the new Spirit-led behavior. Paul continues:

> "So, stop telling lies. Let us tell our neighbors the truth, for we are all parts of the same body. And don't sin by letting anger control you. Don't let the sun go down while you are still angry, for anger gives a foothold to the devil. If you are a thief, quit stealing. Instead, use your hands for good hard work, and

then give generously to others in need. Don't use foul or abusive language. Let everything you say be good and helpful so that your words will be an encouragement to those who hear them. And do not bring sorrow to God's Holy Spirit by the way you live. Remember, he has identified you as his own, guaranteeing that you will be saved on the day of redemption. Get rid of all bitterness, rage, anger, harsh words, and slander, as well as all types of evil behavior. Instead, be kind to each other, tenderhearted, forgiving one another, just as God through Christ has forgiven you" (Ephesians 4:25-32).

SPIRIT-LED IN OUR MINISTRY

God has created you and me to serve Him using what the Bible calls spiritual gifts. God has given every believer at least one spiritual gift: "All these are the work of one and the same Spirit, and He (the Holy Spirit) gives them to each one, just as he determines" (1 Corinthians 12:11).

Spiritual gifts play a large part in God equipping us for service. They are freely given to us by God and are to be used in ministry as a form of serving God. Spiritual gifts are the way God ministers through us by inspiring, energizing, and empowering each of us.

Our capacities, talents, and services are spiritual when they are inspired, led, and empowered by the Holy Spirit.

- **Romans 12.** Paul lists the spiritual gifts as prophesying, serving, teaching, encouraging, contributing, leadership, and mercy.

- **1 Corinthians 12.** Paul includes wisdom, knowledge, faith, healing, miracles, prophecy, discernment, tongues, interpretation of tongues, helps, and administration.

- **Ephesians 4 and 1 Corinthians 12.** Paul lists five equipping positions in the church: apostles, prophets, evangelists, pastors, and teachers.

Each of us should spend time asking God to help us know, understand, and use the spiritual gifts He has given us. Here are three ways you can expand your knowledge about your own personal spiritual gifts.

1. **Spend time in prayer.** You will learn more about your spiritual gifts as you spend time with God in prayer asking Him to show you your gifts. After you finish this lesson, go somewhere alone to be with God. Review your choices and ask God to give you insight. Talk to Him about the gifts. Express any doubt, fear, or frustrations you may have because of this lesson. Ask God for clarity and confirmation.

2. **Investigate.** Investigation is key to knowing and using your spiritual gifts. Like many other things in life, the more you learn, the more you find out how little you really know. We have a workbook called *Wired For Ministry* (available on Amazon) which will help you learn about your own spiritual gifts as well as ministry drives, preferences, and skills.

3. **Do ministry and see what happens.** There is nothing that can substitute for experience. Paul told Timothy to stir up or exercise the gifts that he had. Another way to say that is, "Get out there and try them out." This is the best way to find out what spiritual inclinations God has given you. Get involved in ministry and see where your passions are. If you begin to think your gift is helping, be deliberate by finding ways you can help someone. If your gift is mercy, serve somewhere you can be merciful. If it is faith, meet with your pastor and begin to trust God for accomplishing great things in your church and community. If your spiritual gift is healing, start earnest prayer for sick people. As you get more involved in ministry areas where you think you may have a gift, you will soon find out if this gift is, indeed, a deep passion you have received from God. If it is, experience will help fuel the fire. You will feel alive—as if you found what God really wants you to do—and you have! As you continue to minister, God will help you learn about, modify and grow in your spiritual gifts.

In Galatians 5, Paul writes about choosing to live with the Holy Spirit in control of our lives instead of our old sinful natures: "So, I say, let the Holy Spirit guide your lives. Then you won't be doing what your sinful nature craves" (Galatians 5:16).

In this passage, Paul says that we need to let the Holy Spirit guide our lives. This is being Spirit-led. But how does the Holy Spirit do this? The Holy Spirit gives us the desire to do His will. You will see your spiritual life come alive as you submit yourself to the Holy Spirit each day, asking Him to guide you, shape your desires, and help you live in constant awareness of His presence and power in your life.

INDIVIDUAL EXERCISE
A Healthy Christian is Led by the Spirit

PART 1: SELF-ASSESSMENT

Read each statement below and rate yourself according to the frequency in which that statement is true about you. Be honest with yourself. This is not a pass/fail quiz; it is simply a measuring tool to see where you are in your Christian walk as it relates to being **led by the Spirit**. Don't be afraid to admit that there are some areas where you need to improve. Admitting and committing to change is the way we become and stay spiritually healthy.

I daily seek to be under the influence and led by the Holy Spirit.
☐ regularly   ☐ often   ☐ sometimes   ☐ no

I know what my spiritual gift(s) is, study about it, and use it.
☐ regularly   ☐ often   ☐ sometimes   ☐ no

I keep my conscience clear by confessing sin when needed.
☐ regularly   ☐ often   ☐ sometimes   ☐ no

I spend time in prayer for the needs of others and myself.
☐ regularly   ☐ often   ☐ sometimes   ☐ no

I accept Christ's full forgiveness and unconditional love; my conscience is clean.
☐ regularly   ☐ often   ☐ sometimes   ☐ no

PART 2: HEALTHY CHRISTIAN ACTION PLAN

After you complete the self-assessment, pray and ask God about areas you need to work on. Read the following commitment statement and identify personal goals that will help you achieve being **led by the Spirit** more. Record your goals and monitor your progress as you work toward achieving them. Consider sharing your goals with someone who will support you in your *Healthy Christian* action plan.

Commitment

I commit myself to improving my Christian health by taking the following action steps: I commit myself to improving my Christian health by taking the following action steps:

_____

_____

_____

_____

Bible Verse Resources

Review the Bible resource section in the back of this book. Select two verses that speak to you about being **led by the Spirit** more. Let God speak to you through His Word. Enjoy being with Him. Listen to the truth God wants you to know through these verses. Sense Him speaking to you through them. Claim this biblical truth about you!

1. _____
2. _____

GROUP EXERCISE
A Healthy Christian is Led by the Spirit

Please review the following questions before you meet for group discussion or move on to the next lesson.

DISCUSSION 1

"And I will ask the Father, and he will give you another Counselor to be with you forever—the Spirit of truth. The world cannot accept him, because it neither sees him nor knows him. But you know him, for he lives with you and will be in you" (John 14:16-18).

"Don't you know that you yourselves are God's temple and that God's Spirit lives in you" (1 Corinthians 3:16).

"The Holy Spirit produces this kind of fruit in our lives: love, joy, peace, patience, kindness, goodness, faithfulness, gentleness, and self-control" (Galatians 5:22-23).

"No one has ever seen God; but if we love one another, God lives in us and his love is made complete in us. We know that we live in him and he in us because he has given us of his Spirit" (1 John 4:12-13).

The Bible says that when we are born again that the Holy Spirit lives in us. What evidence is there that this is true? _____

_____

_____

_____

_____

DISCUSSION 2

"Don't be drunk with wine, because that will ruin your life. Instead, be filled with the Holy Spirit" (Ephesians 5:18).

What does it mean to be filled with that Spirit? _____

_____

_____

_____

_____

_____

Is being filled with the Spirit a once for all experience or does it need to be done again and again?

_____

_____

_____

_____

_____

_____

DISCUSSION 3

"All scripture is inspired by God and is useful to teach us what is true and to make us realize what is wrong in our lives. It corrects us when we are wrong and teaches us to do what is right. God uses it to prepare and equip his people to do every good work" (2 Timothy 3:16-17).

How does the Holy Spirit speak to us through the Bible? _____

_____

_____

_____

_____

_____

_____

DISCUSSION 4

What is a spiritual gift? Do you know what your spiritual gift(s) is? _____

_____

_____

_____

_____

_____

DISCUSSION 5

Read the following verse: "Those who live according to the sinful nature have their minds set on what that nature desires, but those who live in accordance with the Spirit have their minds set on what the Spirit desires. The mind of sinful man is death, but the mind controlled by the Spirit is life and peace; the sinful mind is hostile to God. It does not submit to God's law, nor can it do so. Those controlled by the sinful nature cannot please God. You, however, are controlled not by the sinful nature but by the Spirit, if the Spirit of God lives in you. And if anyone does not have the Spirit of Christ, he does not belong to Christ" (Romans 8:5-9).

What should we be doing to allow the Holy Spirit to have influence in our minds? _____

_____

_____

_____

_____

_____

DISCUSSION 6

"Those who belong to Christ Jesus have nailed the passions and desires of their sinful nature to his cross and crucified them there" (Galatians 5:24).

The Holy Spirit convicts us of sin and we have a choice. Do we agree with God and admit that we have done wrong or do we ignore, justify or rationalize it? _____

_____

_____

_____

_____

_____

In many churches, no one wants to admit they have sinned but, instead, act as though everything is fine. How can we change this? How can we create an atmosphere where people can share their personal struggles and get the help they need without judgment? _____

_____

_____

_____

_____

_____

DISCUSSION 7

Why is it important for a church to believe that "There are no perfect people here"? _____

_____

_____

_____

_____

_____

DISCUSSION 8

Share one of the Bible verses you selected from the Bible Verse Resources section that spoke to you about being **led by the Spirit**. How is this verse meaningful to you? _____

_____

_____

_____

_____

_____

5

A Healthy Christian is Outwardly Focused

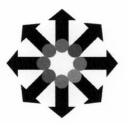

I show compassion to others, work for justice,
and share the gospel message.

A HEALTHY CHRISTIAN
IS OUTWARDLY FOCUSED

The fifth sign of a *Healthy Christian* is that they are outwardly focused. That means that they are on-mission with Jesus—sharing the love of God to those in their community that don't know Jesus. You cannot separate Jesus from His mission. It is why He came to earth. He came to be the Savior of the world. That is something only He could do. It is the same with the church. You cannot separate us from our mission. Jesus came to establish the Church so we could be His hands and feet after He left. He commissioned us to do greater things than He did. It is the mission of the church and its people to live the kind of life that Jesus did. We see this mission with three parts: compassion, justice, and sharing the Gospel message.

I show compassion to others.

Jesus was full of compassion:

> "Jesus traveled through all the towns and villages of that area, teaching in the synagogues and announcing the Good News about the Kingdom. And he healed every kind of disease and illness. When he saw the crowds, he had compassion on them because they were confused and helpless, like sheep without a shepherd. He said to his disciples, 'The harvest is great, but the workers are few. So, pray to the Lord who is in charge of the harvest; ask him to send more workers into his fields'" (Matthew 9:35-38).

Jesus described the kind of ministry He came to do:

> "When he came to the village of Nazareth, his boyhood home, he went as usual to the synagogue on the Sabbath and stood up to read the Scriptures. The scroll of Isaiah the prophet was handed to him. He unrolled the scroll and found the place where this was written: 'The Spirit of the Lord is upon me, for he has anointed me to bring Good News to the poor. He has sent me to proclaim that captives will be released, that the blind will see, that the oppressed will be set free, and that the time of the Lord's favor has come.' He rolled up the scroll, handed it back to the attendant, and sat down. All eyes in the synagogue looked at him intently. Then he began to speak to them. 'The scripture you've just heard has been fulfilled this very day'" (Luke 4:16-21).

This mercy and compassion were expressed in the parable that Jesus shared about the good Samaritan.

"Jesus replied with a story: 'A Jewish man was traveling from Jerusalem down to Jericho, and he was attacked by bandits. They stripped him of his clothes, beat him up, and left him half dead beside the road. By chance, a priest came along. But when he saw the man lying there, he crossed to the other side of the road and passed him by. A Temple assistant walked over and looked at him lying there, but he also passed by on the other side. Then a despised Samaritan came along, and when he saw the man, he felt compassion for him. Going over to him, the Samaritan soothed his wounds with olive oil and wine and bandaged them. Then he put the man on his own donkey and took him to an inn, where he took care of him. The next day he handed the innkeeper two silver coins, telling him, 'Take care of this man. If his bill runs higher than this, I'll pay you the next time I'm here. Now, which of these three would you say was a neighbor to the man who was attacked by bandits?' Jesus asked. The man replied, 'The one who showed him mercy.' Then Jesus said, 'Yes, now go and do the same'" (Luke 10:30-37).

In this parable, Jesus was deliberate in His choice of characters. He purposely chose two religious leaders to be the ones who were not compassionate and a Samaritan, a person from a group that the Jews despised, to be the person who showed the compassion of God.

Why did Jesus tell this story? To correct the misconception that Christianity is to be a religion unto itself, not caring for the rest of the world. It was to wake us up from our apathy and help us see that to be Christ-like we need to be helping those that are hurting on the side of the road in our own neighborhoods. In fact, Jesus was so serious about us helping others that this was the only time Jesus said, "Go and do likewise." This, however, was not the only time the people of God were told that they were overlooking their mandate in loving those outside their circle. God has always cared for the whole world and has always wanted us to be outwardly focused.

In Isaiah 58, God rebukes His people over their ritual of fasting:

"We have fasted before you, they say, and why aren't you impressed? We have been very hard on ourselves, and you don't even notice it! I will tell you why. It's because you are fasting to please yourselves. Even while you fast, you keep oppressing your workers. What good is fasting when you keep on fighting and quarreling? This kind of fasting will never get you anywhere with me. You humble yourselves by going through the motions of penance, bowing your heads like reeds bending in the wind. You dress in burlap and cover yourselves with ashes. Is this what you call fasting? Do you really think this will please the LORD? No, this is the kind of fasting I want: Free those who are wrongly imprisoned; lighten the burden of those who work for you. Let the oppressed go free and remove the chains that bind people. Share your food with the hungry and give shelter to the homeless. Give clothes to those who need them, and do not hide from relatives who need your help" (Isaiah 58:3-7).

This was not an exception. Compassion was part of the Law of Moses. God always intended His people to help those in need. Moses wrote:

> "If there are any poor Israelites in your towns when you arrive in the land the Lord your God is giving you, do not be hard-hearted or tightfisted toward them. Instead, be generous and lend them whatever they need. Do not be mean-spirited and refuse someone a loan because the year for canceling debts is close at hand. If you refuse to make the loan and the needy person cries out to the Lord, you will be considered guilty of sin. Give generously to the poor, not grudgingly, for the Lord your God will bless you in everything you do. There will always be some in the land who are poor. That is why I am commanding you to share freely with the poor and with other Israelites in need" (Deuteronomy 15:7-11).

James described the same responsibility for compassion to the New Testament church:

> "What good is it, dear brothers and sisters, if you say you have faith but don't show it by your actions? Can that kind of faith save anyone? Suppose you see a brother or sister who has no food or clothing, and you say, 'Good-bye and have a good day; stay warm and eat well' but then you don't give that person any food or clothing. What good does that do? So, you see, faith by itself isn't enough. Unless it produces good deeds, it is dead and useless" (James 2:14-17).

If we are going to be serious followers of Jesus Christ, we must look beyond our own needs and look to the needs of others around us. We must exhibit the love and compassion of Christ to those outside the church. Outwardly focused also means we care about justice.

I work for justice.

Justice is a social concept that allows people to co-exist in equity and with righteousness, lawfulness, and moral rightness. Our God is a God of justice. We are repeatedly warned in the Old Testament that we must not pervert justice:

- Do not deny justice to your poor people (Exodus 23:6).
- Do not pervert justice or show partiality (Deuteronomy 16:19).
- The Lord will govern with justice (Psalms 9:8).
- He [God] loves justice (Psalms 11:7).
- Blessed are they who maintain justice (Psalms 106:3).

81

- The Lord secures justice for the poor (Psalms 140:12).
- By justice, a King gives a country stability (Proverbs 29:4).
- Seek justice, encourage the oppressed (Isaiah 1:17).
- For the Lord is a God of justice (Isaiah 30:18).
- Maintain justice and do what is right (Isaiah 56:1).
- Administer true justice (Zechariah 7:9).

The church should act on behalf of those who are being treated unjustly.

- It is unjust that today so many live without or with only marginal health care. Who will advocate? Who will assist clinics that are reaching out to those in need? Will the church step in?

- It is unjust that some in our community go hungry and are homeless while others have a place to sleep and more than enough food. Who will help those who don't have shelter or food to eat? Will the church help?

- It is unjust that there is such a disparity between schools. Federal and state tax dollars can result in quality schools with excellent libraries, computer labs, athletic, and music facilities in some areas and yet, in many urban and rural areas, the schools are woefully inadequate. Who will advocate for quality educational opportunities for all children? Will the church take a stand?

- It is unjust that many cannot find jobs because of inadequate training, job retention skills, or transportation. Who will help with job training, retention, and advancement? Will the church reach out?

- The most segregated hours of the week are Sunday mornings in churches across America. Prejudice and racial discrimination are unjust. Will the church break down the walls?

It is easy to ignore justice when we are not its victims. It is easy to put the blame on those who are the victims. Fighting justice is not easy. It is a deep-rooted problem but if the church will not step up, who will? We must take a serious look at injustice and ask God, "What is my part in this? What can I do? How must I help?" There is no higher calling than to be Christ's disciple of compassion, justice, and the gospel.

I share the Gospel message.

Jesus didn't just heal people, He had a message of salvation that he gave wherever He went: "Jesus traveled through all the towns and villages of that area, teaching in the synagogues and announcing the Good News about the Kingdom. And he healed every kind of disease and illness" (Matthew 9:35).

Jesus taught in the synagogues and wherever else people would listen to Him. People were amazed. They said that He spoke with authority. Others said that they had never heard anyone like Him before. Likewise, a very important part of the church is to preach and teach the Gospel. We must reach out to our neighbors with the Good News and bring up our children in the Christian faith.

There are people all around us waiting to hear the gospel message. They want hope, peace, purpose, and significance. They need Jesus. As a Christian, we need to think outside of the box (and outside the walls of our church) to come up with innovative ways to minister to those around us. Many churches use a woefully low percentage of their annual budget and volunteer hours to reach those outside the church. I know that taking care of the church is important but if we are going to follow Jesus, then we need to delegate a percentage of our church budget and volunteer hours to reach those that don't know the Lord. The early church was not just taking care of themselves, they were actively pursuing new people to get involved. They were on-mission with Jesus by being outwardly focused on those that were outside of their fellowship. How can we reach people around us with the gospel?

OFFER TO PRAY

Although there has been a decrease in people's interest in the church, most people are still interested in spiritual things. There is a multitude of movies with mystical and supernatural themes. People are intrigued by the supernatural. We have an opportunity to open their minds to Christianity by volunteering to pray about issues that matter to them. When offered with sincerity, most people respect this type of outreach. In these situations, when the prayer is answered (and it often is), they are open to knowing more about God. At Mars Hill, the location of one of Paul's most important gospel presentations in Athens, he addressed religious idolatry by noting the Greeks even had an altar to the "Unknown God." So many people today have idols in their minds to an unknown god just sitting there getting dusty. They need us to pray with them, revealing the uselessness of their idol, and illustrating who God really is.

BE A GOOD NEIGHBOR

I was challenged once by a speaker who drew a square grid made up of three rows and three columns, much like a tic-tac-toe game. He put an "X" in the center and said it represented "home." The other squares, he explained, represented the houses right around you. He instructed us to fill in each square with our neighbors' names and everything we knew about them. How horrifying and embarrassing! I hardly knew anything about my own neighbors next door. What a challenge for me. I have a mission field right around my house and I know nothing about any of them. How could I ever expect to be a witness to them? Since then, I have been more purposeful in getting to know them. I had the honor of doing the funeral for one of my neighbors right in his backyard with all the neighborhood there.

There are many ways to get to know your neighbors. Here are a few:
- Watch for times of need and be ready to help
- Be thoughtful when someone is sick

- Share some food with a neighbor
- Give a small gift during a holiday
- Go to a sports game of one of the children in the neighborhood
- Help with a neighborhood picnic

Neighboring isn't necessarily sharing the gospel, but it is building a relationship from which you could talk about spiritual things.

ASK QUESTIONS, THEN LISTEN

We may believe that people don't want to talk about God or Christianity. What I think most people object to is having the gospel—or anything for that matter—shoved at them. It is true that Jesus claims that he is the only way to heaven. That, of course, can upset people who don't agree. But it is not Jesus that they are upset with; it's the statement itself. To a secular mind, Jesus' claim of being the only way isn't tolerant of other religions and beliefs. That is true. From a purely intellectual argument, it is biased. But it isn't meant to be looked at from a philosophical view. It is spiritual. And when you consider how Christianity solves our spiritual needs, what Jesus said makes total sense. That is why asking questions that get to spiritual issues opens hearts to hear the gospel.

But it is not just asking questions. We need to listen to what they have to say. People are starving for good relationships. They want to have people in their lives that care. A neighbor should be someone like that. Asking people about their lives is always a welcome discussion. Asking about their children, their favorite sport, hobby, or civic organization is usually an acceptable conversation. As you listen, trust is built on their end and you begin to care more about them in your own heart. When those two attitudes start working together, you have an atmosphere conducive to witnessing. It won't take long for the discussion to turn to needs. And then, like a neighbor who is asked for a cup of sugar, you can go to your cupboard of experience and share how you have been comforted in your own time of need. This is what the Bible means when it tells us to comfort others in the way we have been comforted.

Christianity doesn't make sense to the average person who doesn't know Jesus. It is only through their own needs that they start to hunger for something more. Getting to know and care for our neighbors through interesting and exciting conversations will allow them to see how God meets your needs and to consider inviting God to meet theirs.

INVITE OTHERS TO CHURCH SERVICES AND ACTIVITIES

As a church, we need to think of things that we can get the neighborhood to come to. Most people haven't stepped foot in a church in years. If they did, it was probably for a wedding, infant baptism, or funeral. That is why turning our attention to creating interesting children's programs, festivals, sports programs, affinity programs, dinners, special speakers, and interesting sermon series is a good way to invest our resources. Church services and events, along with genuine excitement and commitment from everyone in the church will result in effective outreach. Pastors can't make this happen by themselves—they need committed and engaged congregants to help support and orchestrate systematic, intentional and outwardly focused outreach.

In John 4, Jesus was talking with a woman at a well. She was deeply moved by her discussion with Him: "Then, leaving her water jar, the woman went back to the town and said to the people, 'Come, see a man who told me everything I ever did. Could this be the Messiah?' They came out of the town and made their way toward him" (John 4:28-30).

This is a great example of a person inviting people to come and see for themselves. We need to be more proactive in thinking about programs and events that we can invite people to—things that we can be excited about like the woman at the well.

INVITE OTHERS TO YOUR HOME

On a personal level, it can be sharing about some of the excellent Christian books and movies that are out today that you are excited about. It can also be sharing some of the music or Christian radio stations. There are excellent vehicles of the gospel that we can invite them to consider without embarrassment. Rather than leaving it to chance that they will view, read, or listen to what you have suggested, invite them to your home with some others to share opinions on the book, video, or movie you told them about. To do this you need to be a good listener. Asking good discussion questions while respecting everyone's answers is a great way to create spiritual thirst.

It is best to find something that you like and are comfortable with so you can be enthusiastic about it; something that can speak for itself, so you don't have to defend it. There were people who disagreed with Jesus so don't be surprised if people express contrary arguments. Respectfully listen and thank them. They are your friends and you can love them even though they disagree with you. But don't worry. Remember, it took a conversation before Jesus was able to zero in on the woman at the well. Likewise, materials on contemporary issues and felt needs are great ways to get a discussion going and bringing them a step closer to knowing God.

In the United States, there are over 190,000 evangelical and conservative Protestant congregations with over 43,000,000 congregants. Add to that, 77,000 mainline Protestant congregations with 22,000,000 congregants. That is 65,000,000 people! That is more than enough people to make a significant difference, but we can't sit around and think everyone else will do it.

We must act! Will you and your church go outside your comfort zone and work in those communities around you to help those in need with compassion, justice, and the gospel message?

We need a mind shift. For too long, churches have been trying to be the best church in the community. We have compared ourselves with other churches. But is that the right measuring stick? Is that what God wants? Perhaps there are better metrics.

Maybe we should quit striving to be the best church *in* and become, as the author Eric Swanson suggests, the best church *for* the community. You can read about it in his book, *The Externally Focused Quest: Becoming the Best Church for the Community.* Since he wrote that book he has even gone further and has said that we should be the best church *with* the community. In his writings, Eric asks a sobering question that we need to consider: "If your church were to close its doors, would anyone in the community be upset?" It is a serious question and one that we may not like the answer to. But here is the good news. It is not too late!

We can still make a difference. We can embrace our mission to be a true community church by considering ways we can be the hands and feet of Jesus right where we worship. We can take on a new mantra—one that says, "Yes we want to be the best church for and with the community."

INDIVIDUAL EXERCISE
A Healthy Christian is Outwardly Focused

PART 1: SELF-ASSESSMENT

Read each statement below and rate yourself according to the frequency in which that statement is true about you. Be honest with yourself. This is not a pass/fail quiz; it is simply a measuring tool to see where you are in your Christian walk as it relates to being **outwardly focused**. Don't be afraid to admit that there are some areas where you need to improve. Admitting and committing to change is the way we become and stay spiritually healthy.

I am involved in a ministry.

☐ regularly   ☐ often   ☐ sometimes   ☐ no

I volunteer when needed for extra duties at church.

☐ regularly   ☐ often   ☐ sometimes   ☐ no

I meet the needs of the needy when called upon.

☐ regularly   ☐ often   ☐ sometimes   ☐ no

I invite people to church services and activities.

☐ regularly   ☐ often   ☐ sometimes   ☐ no

I share literature and other witnessing tools with people outside the church.

☐ regularly   ☐ often   ☐ sometimes   ☐ no

I share my own testimony of God's active role in my life with others.

☐ regularly   ☐ often   ☐ sometimes   ☐ no

I share the gospel message with those that do not know it.

☐ regularly   ☐ often   ☐ sometimes   ☐ no

I have led someone to the Lord in the last two years.

☐ regularly   ☐ often   ☐ sometimes   ☐ no

PART 2: HEALTHY CHRISTIAN ACTION PLAN

After you complete the self-assessment, pray and ask God about areas you need to work on. Read the following commitment statement and identify personal goals that will help you achieve being more outwardly focused. Record your goals and monitor your progress as you work toward achieving them. Consider sharing your goals with someone who will support you in your Healthy Christian action plan.

Commitment

I commit myself to improving my Christian health by taking the following action steps: I commit myself to improving my Christian health by taking the following action steps:

_____

_____

_____

_____

_____

Bible Verse Resources

Review the Bible resource section in the back of this book. Select two verses that speak to you about being **outwardly focused**. Let God speak to you through His Word. Enjoy being with Him. Listen to the truth God wants you to know through these verses. Sense Him speaking to you through them. Claim this biblical truth about you!

1. _____
2. _____

GROUP DISCUSSION
A Healthy Christian is Outwardly Focused

Please review the following questions before you meet for group discussion or move on to the next lesson.

DISCUSSION 1

After the story of the Good Samaritan, Jesus said: "'Now which of these three do you think was a neighbor to the man who was beaten by the robbers?' The man who knew the Law said, 'The one who showed loving-pity on him.' Then Jesus said, 'Go and do the same'" (Luke 10:36-37).

What does God want us to do? _____

_____

_____

_____

_____

_____

_____

_____

DISCUSSION 2

"Is not the time without eating which I choose, a time to take off the chains of sin, and to take the heavy load of sin off the neck? Is it not a time to let those who suffer under a sinful power go free, and to break every load from their neck? Is it not a time to share your food with the hungry, and bring the poor man into your house who has no home of his own? Is it not a time to give clothes to the person you see who has no clothes, and a time not to hide yourself from your own family? Then your light will break out like the early morning, and you will soon be healed. Your right and good works will go before you. And the shining-greatness of the Lord will keep watch behind you" (Isaiah 58:6-8).

Why was God upset with the people's fasting? What did He want them to do instead? _____

_____

_____

_____

_____

_____

_____

_____

DISCUSSION 3

James writes: "So, you see, faith by itself isn't enough. Unless it produces good deeds, it is dead and useless" (James 2:17).

What is James talking about? _____
_____
_____
_____
_____
_____

Does this apply to the church today? _____
_____
_____
_____
_____
_____

DISCUSSION 4

The Bible gives many examples of justice.
- Do not deny justice to your poor people (Exodus 23:6).
- Do not pervert justice or show partiality (Deuteronomy 16:19).
- The Lord will govern with justice (Psalms 9:8).
- He [God] loves justice (Psalms 11:7).
- Blessed are they who maintain justice (Psalms 106:3).
- The Lord secures justice for the poor (Psalms 140:12).
- By justice, a King gives a country stability (Proverbs 29:4).
- Seek justice, encourage the oppressed (Isaiah 1:17).
- For the Lord is a God of justice (Isaiah 30:18).
- Maintain justice and do what is right (Isaiah 56:1).
- Administer true justice (Zechariah 7:9).

Why is justice so important to God? _____
_____
_____
_____
_____
_____
_____

Where can you and your church be involved in justice in your surrounding area? _____
_____
_____
_____
_____
_____

DISCUSSION 5

How well do you know your neighbors? Do you know the names of the people in your "tic-tac-toe" box, where they work and other interesting facts? _____
_____
_____
_____
_____
_____

What are some ways that you think you could be a good neighbor where you live? _____
_____
_____
_____
_____
_____
_____

Does it frighten you to engage with your neighbors about your faith? What type of questions would be easy for you to ask? _____
_____
_____
_____
_____
_____

We often talk about sports, movies, children, and politics but when it comes to Christianity it can be hard to start a conversation. Why is this? _____
_____
_____
_____
_____
_____
_____

Can you think of any Christian topics that would be good to share with your neighbors? _____

_____

_____

_____

_____

_____

_____

DISCUSSION 6

To what kind of programs, events or sermon series would you feel comfortable inviting your friends, neighbors, co-workers or relatives? _____

_____

_____

_____

_____

_____

_____

DISCUSSION 7

What are some ways we can be the best church *for* and *with* our community? _____

_____

_____

_____

_____

_____

_____

DISCUSSION 8

Share one of the verses you selected from the Bible Verse Resources section that spoke to you about being **outwardly focused**. How is this verse meaningful to you? _____

_____

_____

_____

_____

_____

Closing

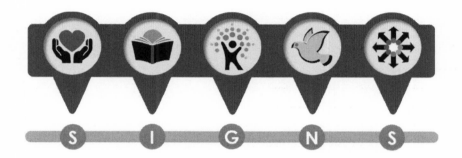

We can be the best church for
and with the community. It all begins with
Healthy Christians.

CLOSING

The purpose of this book is to be a catalyst—to spark a fire that will begin to take over your life. A desire to love Jesus, love God's word, be emotionally resilient, led by the Holy Spirit and outwardly focused…this is just the beginning!

Where do you go from here? I suggest that you go back and look at the commitments you made at the end of each chapter. Let God speak to your heart, then commit yourself to making a change. We would love to join you on your journey of following Christ!

Find out more at the Empower Ministry website: www.empowerminstry.org.

Bible Verse Resources

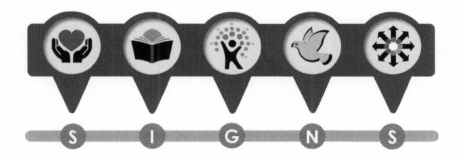

If you want to know what God thinks about you,
meditate on Bible verses and let God speak to you through
His Word. This is the biblical truth about you!

BIBLE VERSE RESOURCES

Meditations

BIBLE VERSES QUOTED FROM STANDARD TRANSLATIONS

God gives me peace. "You will keep in perfect peace all who trust in you, all whose thoughts are fixed on you. Trust in the Lord always, for the Lord God is the eternal Rock" (Isaiah 26:3-4, *NLT*).

God takes delight in me. "The Lord your God is with you, he is mighty to save. He will take great delight in you, he will quiet you with his love, he will rejoice over you with singing" (Zephaniah 3:17, *NIV*).

I put my trust in God. "Let the morning bring me word of your unfailing love, for I have put my trust in you. Show me the way I should go, for to you I lift up my soul. Rescue me from my enemies, O Lord, for I hide myself in you. Teach me to do your will, for you are my God; may your good Spirit lead me on level ground" (Psalms 143:8, 10, *NIV*).

I will not be afraid. "So, we say with confidence, The Lord is my helper; I will not be afraid. What can man do to me?" (Hebrews 13:6, *NIV*).

I am His child; I will never be forsaken by God. "God has said, 'Never will I leave you; never will I forsake you'" (Hebrews 13:5, *NIV*).

I come boldly to the throne of our gracious God. "So then, since we have a great High Priest who has entered heaven, Jesus the Son of God, let us hold firmly to what we believe. This High Priest of ours understands our weaknesses, for he faced all of the same testings we do, yet he did not sin. So, let us come boldly to the throne of our gracious God. There we will receive his mercy, and we will find grace to help us when we need it most" (Hebrew 4:14-16, *NLT*).

I live in God's perfect peace. "You will keep in perfect peace all who trust in you, all whose thoughts are fixed on you" (Isaiah 26:3, *NLT*).

God's Holy Spirit lives in me. "I pray that out of his glorious riches he may strengthen you with power through his Spirit in your inner being" (Ephesians 3:16, *NIV*).

God comforts me. "For when we came into Macedonia, this body of ours had no rest, but we were harassed at every turn—conflicts on the outside, fears within. But God, who comforts the downcast, comforted us by the coming of Titus" (2 Corinthians 7:5-6, *NIV*).

Jesus makes me whole. "When Jesus saw him lying there and learned that he had been in this condition for a long time, he asked him, 'Do you want to get well?'" (John 5:6, *NIV*).

I live in God's presence, in His life-giving light. "You have kept my feet from slipping. So now I can walk in your presence, O God, in your life-giving light" (Psalms 56:13, *NIV*).

God loves me. "I have loved you even as the Father has loved me. Remain in my love" (John 15:9, *NLT*).

My hope is in the living God. "And so, Lord, where do I put my hope? My only hope is in you" (Psalms 39:7, *NLT*).

I have fellowship with God. "Come close to God, and God will come close to you" (James 4:8, *NLT*).

I am chosen by God to be His ambassador of love. "So, as those who have been chosen of God, holy and beloved, put on a heart of compassion, kindness, humility, gentleness, and patience; bearing with one another, and forgiving each other, whoever has a complaint against anyone; just as the Lord forgave you, so also should you" (Colossians 3:12-13, *NASB*).

I am God's prized procession. "He chose to give birth to us by giving us his true word. And we, out of all creation, became his prized possession" (James 1:18, *NLT*).

I live in forgiveness and freedom. "If we claim we have no sin, we are only fooling ourselves and not living in the truth. But if we confess our sins to him, he is faithful and just to forgive us our sins and to cleanse us from all wickedness" (1 John 1:8-9, *NLT*).

Christ's peace rules in my heart. "Let the peace of Christ rule in your hearts, since as members of one body you were called to peace. And be thankful" (Colossians 3:15, *NIV*).

I find shelter in God's presence. "You hide them in the shelter of your presence" (Psalms 31:20, *NLT*).

I am trusting God. "But I am trusting you, O Lord, saying, you are my God. My future is in your hands" (Psalms 31:14-15, *NLT*).

I am loved unconditionally. "Remember me in the light of your unfailing love, for you are merciful, O Lord" (Psalms 25:7, *NLT*).

I am loved by our Holy God. "And so, dear brothers and sisters, we can boldly enter heaven's Most Holy Place because of the blood of Jesus. By his death, Jesus opened a new and life-giving way through the curtain into the Most Holy Place. And since we have a great High Priest who rules over God's house, let us go right into the presence of God with sincere hearts fully trusting him" (Hebrews 10:19-22, *NLT*).

Affirmations

BIBLE VERSES PARAPHRASED IN THE FIRST PERSON

God pursues me. It is true that God's pursues me with His goodness and his unfailing love every day of my life (Psalm 23:6).

The Lord is close. When I am brokenhearted, the Lord is close to comfort me. When my spirit is crushed, He rescues me (Psalm 34:18).

I am His. God has called me by name; I am His (Isaiah 43:1).

The Lord gives me power. The Lord gives me power when I am weary and increases my strength when I am weak (Isaiah 40:29).

God is doing a new thing. I will forget the past and not dwell on it. Instead, I can see that God is doing a new thing (Isaiah 43:18).

God is the source of all my comfort. I praise God, the Father of our Lord Jesus Christ, who is my merciful Father and the source of all my comfort (2 Corinthians 1:3).

God calls me to talk with Him. Lord, in my heart I have heard You say, "Come, talk with me." My heart shouts, "Yes, Lord, I am coming!" (Psalm 27:8).

I am a delight. The Lord delights in me (Psalm 149:4).

Love is overflowing in my life. With God's help, love is overflowing in my life and I am growing in knowledge and understanding (Philippians 1:9).

Christ gives me strength. I can do everything through Christ, who gives me strength (Philippians 4:13).

I am committed to doing good deeds. Christ gave His life to free me from every kind of sin. He cleanses me, making me His very own and totally committed to doing good deeds (Titus 2:14).

I am valuable to God. I am valuable to God, so I won't be afraid. He will take care of me (Luke 12:7).

I overflow with deep joy. Jesus loves me as much as His Father loves him. I believe this and focus on His love. I overflow with deep joy! (John 15:9,11).

I am a child of God. I have believed in Jesus and accepted him. He, therefore, gave me the privilege of becoming a child of God (John 1:12).

I am a new person. I belong to Christ and I am a new person. My old life is gone, and now I am living a new life (2 Corinthians 5:17).

God chose me. Before God made the world, He loved me and chose me in Christ to be holy and without fault in his eyes (Ephesians 1:4).

God's love completes me. Even though it is too great to fully understand, the life and power that comes from experiencing the love of Christ completes me (Ephesians 3:19).

I must live a worthy life. I must live a life worthy of the calling God has made in my life (Ephesians 4:1).

The Fruit of the Spirit can be mine. I want the Holy Spirit to produce its fruit in my life. The fruit is love, joy, peace, patience, kindness, goodness, faithfulness, gentleness, and self-control (Galatians 5:22-23).

I have God's compassion and favor. For it is through God's remarkable compassion and favor, his grace, that I have been delivered from judgment and given eternal life. It was nothing I have done. It is a gift from God, so I can't take any credit for it (Ephesians 2:8-9).

I am God's masterpiece. I am the result of God's creation, a new masterpiece created through my relationship with Jesus Christ. He planned a long time ago that I would live for him and do the good he has called me to do (Ephesians 2:10).

I am a person of light. For once I was full of darkness, but now I have the light of the Lord in me. So, I will live as a person of light doing being careful to know what pleases the Lord and doing right. I will not participate in the worthless deeds of evil and darkness; instead, I will expose them (Ephesians 5:8-11).

I will live with wisdom. I will be careful how I live. I don't want to live like a fool but rather, live with wisdom. I will make the most of all the opportunities God has given me. I won't act thoughtlessly but will try to ascertain what the Lord wants me to do. I won't let substance take over my life because it will ruin it. Instead, I will seek to be filled with the Holy Spirit (Ephesians 5:15-18).

I am God's child. I do not have to be afraid of God for I have received God's Spirit. He has made me his child and I now affectionately call him, "Daddy; Father." God's Spirit joins with my spirit assuring me that I am his child (Romans 8:15-16).

God is with me. I will not be afraid or discouraged because the Lord Himself goes before me. He is with me and will never leave me or forsake me (Deuteronomy 3:18).

God will never abandon me. I will be strong and courageous! I won't be afraid or full of terror. I won't panic because You Lord, my God, will personally go ahead of me. You will not fail. You will never abandon me (Deuteronomy 31:6).

God gives me strength. Almighty God, You give me strength. You are my God. You save me. You are my Heavenly Father. I will praise and exalt You! (Exodus 15:2).

I am a conqueror. I am more than a conqueror through Christ who loves me (Romans 8:37).

I am in God's presence. I seek for You, Lord, and Your strength. I desperately seek Your face, so I can be continuously in Your presence (1 Chronicles 16:11).

God's strength keeps me from falling. Even when I stumble, Your words, Lord, uphold me. You strengthen my legs and keep me from falling (Job 4:4).

The Lord makes me safe. I lie down and sleep because You alone, Lord, make me safe (Psalm 4:8).

I will not be afraid for God is with me. Even if I walk through the darkest valley, I will not fear for You are right here with me. Your rod and staff comfort and protect me. You have prepared a feast for me in the presence of my enemies. You honor me by anointing my head with oil. Truly my cup overflows with blessings (Psalm 23:4-5).

God protects me with His love. Lord, I rejoice in You. I am blessed. I am full of joy and singing because I take refuge in You. You protect me with Your shield of love (Psalm 5:11-12).

God's power delivers me from my troubles. I love You, Lord, for You are my strength, rock, fortress, deliverer, refuge, and shield. You are the power that delivers me from my troubles. In your presence, I find safety (Psalm 18:1-2).

God sees my troubles and cares about my anguish. I rejoice in God's unfailing love for He sees my troubles and cares about the anguish of my soul (Psalm 31:7).

The Lord is tender and compassionate toward me. The Lord is like a father to me; tender and compassionate (Psalm 103:13).

God's plans for my life will work out. All God's plans for my life will work out because His faithful love endures forever (Psalm 138:8).

God's love is unfailing. I trust in God and meditate on His unfailing love for me each morning (Psalm 143:8).

God's perfect love casts out my fear. I have no fear because God's perfect love casts out all fear (1 John 4:18).

God is gracious and merciful. I know that God is a God of forgiveness. He is gracious and merciful, slow to become angry, and rich in unfailing love. He will not abandon me (Nehemiah 14:18).

God helps me in times of trouble. God is my refuge and strength; He is always ready to help me in times of trouble. So, I will not fear (Psalm 46:1-2).

I am content. I have learned how to be content with whatever I have. I know how to live with almost nothing or with everything. I have learned this secret of living in every situation, whether it is with being full or hungry, with a lot of provisions or very little. Here is the secret—I can do everything through Christ, who gives me strength (Philippians 4:11-13).

My hope is in the Lord. I will be strong and take heart, for I hope in the Lord (Psalm 31:24).

The Lord is my helper. I can say with confidence that the Lord is my helper. I will not be afraid of what man can do to me (Hebrew 13:6).

I have peace of mind and heart. Jesus has given me a gift—deep peace of mind and heart. This is a peace the world could never give me. So, now I do not need to be troubled or afraid (John 14:27).

God protects me and gives me comfort. When I walk through a dark valley, I will choose not to be afraid. I can do this because You, O Lord, are close beside me. Like a shepherd with rod and staff, You protect me and give me comfort (Psalm 23:4).

Nothing will separate me from God's love. I am convinced that nothing can ever separate me from God's love. Not death nor life, angels nor demons, fears for today or our worries about tomorrow—not even the powers of hell can separate me from God's love. Not power above or below the earth—indeed, nothing in all creation will ever be able to separate me from the love that God has for me, revealed in Christ Jesus our Lord (Romans 8:38-39).

Believing What God Believes About Me

BIBLICAL PRINCIPLES PARAPHRASED

I am a new person with a new life. Before God made the world, He loved me and chose me in Christ to be holy and without fault in His eyes. God decided in advance to adopt me into His family by bringing me to Himself through Jesus Christ. This is what He wanted to do, and it gave Him great pleasure. So, I praise God for the glorious grace He has poured out to me.

He is so rich in kindness and grace that He purchased my freedom with the blood of His Son and forgave me all my sins. He has showered His kindness on me, along with all wisdom and understanding. For God so loved the world that He gave His one and only Son, Jesus, so when I became a believer in Him, I will no longer have to fear eternal death, but now have eternal life. When I came to Christ and received Him as my Savior and Lord, I became a new person. The old life was gone; a new life began! I have been transformed into a new creation. He washed away my sins, giving me a new birth and new life through the Holy Spirit. So, I am letting God transform me into a new person by changing the way I think. My inward being is being renewed day by day. In fact, I am throwing off my old sinful nature and my former way of life, which is corrupted by lust and deception. Instead, I am letting the Holy Spirit renew my thoughts and attitudes. I will put on my new nature and be renewed as I learn to know my Creator and become like Him. God has given me everything I need for living a godly life. REFERENCE VERSES: Ephesians 1: 4-8; John 3:16-17; Romans 7; Romans 5:11; 2 Corinthians 5:17; Galatians 6:15; Titus 3:5; Romans 12:2; 2 Corinthians 4:16; Ephesians 4:22-23; Colossians 3:10; and 2 Peter 1:3.

I have life through God's Holy Spirit. The Holy Spirit helps me know the wonderful things God has freely given me. In fact, I am a temple of the living God and His Spirit lives in me. For I know how dearly God loves me because He has given me the Holy Spirit to fill my heart with His love. And the Holy Spirit is Christ's advocate to help me and be with me forever. This advocate, the Holy Spirit, who God sent in the name of Jesus, teaches me all things and reminds me of everything that Jesus wants me to know. The Spirit of God, who raised Jesus from the dead, lives in me and the Holy Spirit helps me with my weaknesses. When I don't know what to pray for, the Holy Spirit Himself intercedes for me with God the Father. The Holy Spirit prays for me with groanings that cannot be expressed in words. And my Heavenly Father knows what the Spirit is saying, for the Spirit pleads for me in harmony with God's own will. So, I know that God causes everything to work together for the good because God loves me and has called me according to his purpose for me.   REFERENCE VERSES: 1 Corinthians 2:12, 1 Corinthians 3:16, Romans 5:5, John 14:16-17, Romans 8:11, and Romans 26-28.

I live in grace without condemnation. Since I have been made right in God's sight by faith, I have peace with God because of what Jesus Christ, my Savior, and Lord, has done for me. Because of my faith, Christ has brought me to this place of grace, an undeserved privilege, where I now stand. For God did not send his Son into the world to condemn me but to save me through Him, so by believing in Him, I will never be condemned. When I was utterly helpless, Christ came at just the right time and died on the cross for me. God showed His great love for me by sending Christ to die for me while I was still sinning. But since I have been made right in God's sight by the blood of Christ, He will certainly save me from God's condemnation. I do not let sin control the way I live; with Christ's help, I do not have to give in to sinful desires. I don't have to let any part of my body become an instrument of evil to serve sin. Instead, I will continually give myself completely to God, for I was dead but now I have new life. So, I will use my whole body as an instrument to do what is right for the glory of God. Sin is no longer my master, for I live in the freedom of God's grace. So now there is

105

no condemnation for me because I belong to Christ Jesus. And because I belong to Him, the power of the life-giving Spirit has freed me from the power of sin that leads to death. REFERENCE VERSES: Romans 5:1-2, 6-10, Romans 6:12-14, and Romans 8:1-2.

God has called me to be a new holy person. I am careful not to claim that I am without sin. If I do, I am simply deceiving myself and I am not being truthful Instead, if I confess my sins, God is faithful and just and will forgive me of all my sins and purify me from all unrighteousness. I have been called by God to be his own holy person. He made me made right with God; pure and holy. God has freed me from sin, making me holy by means of Christ Jesus. I have been made right in God's sight by faith, and now I have peace with God because of what Jesus Christ my Lord has done for me. Because of my faith, Christ has brought me into this place of undeserved privilege where I now stand, and I confidently and joyfully look forward to sharing God's glory. Because God is rich in mercy and has a great love for me, He has made me alive with Christ even though I was dead in transgressions. I have decided to give my body and mind to God because of all he has done for me. I want it to be a living and holy sacrifice—the kind God will find acceptable. So, I won't copy the behavior and customs of this world, but instead, I am letting God transform me into a new person by changing the way I think. This way I will learn to know God's will for me, which is good and pleasing and perfect. It is by His grace that I have been saved through faith—and this is not because of me, it is a gift from God— It is not by my doing good, so I cannot boast. REFERENCE VERSES: 1 John 1:8-9, 1 Corinthians 1:2, 1 Corinthians 1:30, Romans 5:1-2, Romans 12:1-2, and Ephesians 2:4-9.

Christ helps me live my life. I rejoice when I run into problems and trials, for I know that they help me develop endurance. And endurance develops strength of character. So, I make every effort to add to my faith goodness; and to goodness, knowledge; and to knowledge, self-control; and to self-control, perseverance; and to perseverance, godliness; and to godliness, mutual affection; and to mutual affection, love. For when I possess these qualities in increasing measure, they will keep me from being ineffective and unproductive in my knowledge of our Lord Jesus Christ. I do not have to let my heart become troubled because I believe in God. And God has not given me a spirit of fear and timidity, but of power, love, and self-discipline. Jesus gives me peace, not the kind the world gives. So, I do not have to let my heart be troubled or afraid. So, I consider it pure joy whenever I face trials because I know that the testing of my faith produces perseverance making me mature and complete, not lacking anything. I know that if I lack wisdom, I need to quit doubting and simply ask God, who will give it to me. I am more than a conqueror through him who loved us. If I am afraid I call on you for you are there, your rod and staff protect and comfort me like a good shepherd does for his sheep. For I am convinced that neither death nor life, neither angels nor demons, neither the present nor the future, nor any powers, neither height nor depth, nor anything else in all creation, will be able to separate me from the love of God that is in Christ Jesus my Lord. REFERENCE VERSES: Romans 5:3-4, 2 Peter 1:5-8, John 14:1, 27, 2 Timothy 1:7, James 1:2-6, Psalms 23: 4, and Romans 8:37-39.

God gives victory in spiritual battle. I use God's mighty weapons, not worldly weapons, to knock down the strongholds of human reasoning and to destroy false arguments. For I am strong in the Lord and in his mighty power. I put on the full armor of God, so take my stand against the devil's schemes. For my struggle is not against flesh and blood, but against the rulers, against the authorities, against the powers of this dark world and against the spiritual forces of evil in the heavenly realms. Therefore, I put on the full armor of God, so I can stand my ground, and after I have done everything, to stand, I will stand firm with the belt of truth buckled around my waist, the breastplate of righteousness in place, and my feet fitted with the readiness that comes from the gospel of peace. And then I take up the shield of faith, with which I can extinguish all the flaming arrows of the evil one, along with the helmet of salvation and the sword of the Spirit, which is the word of God. For he has rescued me from the dominion of darkness and brought me into the kingdom of the Son he loves, in whom I have redemption, the forgiveness of sins. REFERENCE VERSES: 2 Corinthians 10:4, Ephesians 6:10-17, and Colossians 1:13-14.

Our mission is to love others. Jesus said, "As the Father has loved me, so have I loved you. Now remain in my love. If you keep my commands, you will remain in my love, just as I have kept my Father's commands and remain in his love. I have told you this so that my joy may be in you and that your joy may be complete. My command is this: Love each other as I have loved you. I am careful not to merely listen to the word, and so deceive yourselves but I strive to do what it says. I don't just say I have faith, I show it by doing good in His name. I am always prepared to give a gentle and respectful answer to everyone who asks me to give the reason for the hope that I have. In fact, as God, the Father of my Lord Jesus Christ, the Father of compassion and the God of all comfort, comforts me in all my troubles, I will go and comfort those in any trouble with the same comfort I received from God. REFERENCE VERSES: John 15:9-12, James 1:22; James 2:18, 1 Peter 3:15, and 2 Corinthians 1:3-4.

God will help me as I live for Him. For I am God's masterpiece. He has created me anew in Christ Jesus, so I can do the good things he planned for me long ago. So I keep on asking God to enable me to live a life worthy of His call. May He give me the power to accomplish all the good things my faith prompts me to do. Then the name of our Lord Jesus will be honored because of the way I live. This is all made possible because of the grace of our God and Lord, Jesus Christ. I rejoice even though I have had to suffer grief in all kinds of trials, it has resulted in purifying my faith—which is of greater worth than gold, which perishes even though refined by fire. Faith, so though I have never seen Christ, I love Him; and am filled with an inexpressible and glorious joy. The LORD is my light and my salvation— whom shall I fear? The LORD is the stronghold of my life— of whom shall I be afraid? I can cast all my anxiety on God because He cares for me. I will always be full of joy in the Lord. I won't worry about anything; instead, I will pray about everything. I will tell God what I need and thank Him for all He has done and then I will experience God's peace, which exceeds anything I can understand. His peace will guard my hearts and minds as I live in Christ Jesus. I will fix my thoughts on what is true, honorable, right, pure, lovely, admirable, excellent and worthy of praise. As I do this our God of peace will be with me. I am learning to be content with whatever I have. I know how to live on almost nothing or with everything. I have learned the secret of living in every situation, whether it is with a full stomach or empty, with plenty or little. For I can do everything through Christ, who gives me strength. God will meet all my needs according to the riches of His glory in Christ Jesus. God will keep me in perfect peace as I trust in Him and fix my thoughts on Him! So I won't be afraid, for God is with me. He will hold me up with His victorious right hand. I won't be discouraged, for He is my God. He will strengthen me and help me. This I know, Christ is with me, even to the end of time. REFERENCE VERSES: Ephesians 2:10, 2 Thessalonians 1:11-12, 1 Peter 1:6-9, Psalms 27:1, 1 Peter 5:7, Philippians 4:6-19, Isaiah 26:3, and Matthew 28:20.

God has given His wisdom, peace, power, and protection to me. I ask God, the glorious Father of our Lord Jesus Christ, to give me spiritual wisdom and insight so that I might grow in my knowledge of God. I pray that my heart will be flooded with light so that I can understand the confident hope Christ has given to those He called—His holy people who are His rich and glorious inheritance, and I am one of them! I pray that I will understand the incredible greatness of God's power for me because I believe in Him. This is the same mighty power that raised Christ from the dead and seated Him in the place of honor at God's right hand in the heavenly realms. Now He is far above any ruler or authority or power or leader or anything else—not only in this world but also in the world to come. And God has put all things under the authority of Christ and has made Him head over all things for the benefit of the church. Praise the Lord! For he has heard my cry for mercy. The Lord is my strength and shield. I trust him with all my heart. He helps me, and my heart is filled with joy. You will keep me in perfect peace because I trust in Him because my thoughts are fixed on Him! God the Father and Christ Jesus my Lord gives me grace, mercy, and peace. The Lord Jesus Christ Himself and God our Father, who loves me and by His grace gave me eternal comfort and a wonderful hope, He will continue to comfort me and strengthen me in every good thing I do and say.   REFERENCE VERSES: Ephesians 1:17-23, Psalms 28:6-8, Isaiah 26:3, 2 Timothy 1:2, and 2 Thessalonians 2:16-17.

BIBLICAL PRINCIPLES IN BIBLE VERSES

God gives me peace. "You will keep in perfect peace all who trust in you, all whose thoughts are fixed on you! Trust in the Lord always, for the Lord God is the eternal Rock" (Isaiah 26:3-4, *NLT*).

God delights in me. "The Lord your God is with you, he is mighty to save. He will take great delight in you, he will quiet you with his love, he will rejoice over you with singing" (Zephaniah 3:17, *NIV*)

God daily renews my heart and mind. "Therefore, we do not lose heart. Though outwardly we are wasting away, yet inwardly we are being renewed day by day" (2 Corinthians 4:16, *NIV*).

God shows me the way to go. "Let the morning bring me word of your unfailing love, for I have put my trust in you. Show me the way I should go, for to you I lift up my soul. Rescue me from my enemies, O Lord, for I hide myself in you. Teach me to do your will, for you are my God; may your good Spirit lead me on level ground" (Psalms 143:8,10, *NIV*).

God cares for me when I am in need. "The Lord gives justice to the oppressed and food to the hungry. The Lord frees the prisoners. The Lord opens the eyes of the blind. The Lord lifts up those who are weighed down. The Lord loves the godly. The Lord protects the foreigners among us. He cares for the orphans and widows, but he frustrates the plans of the wicked" (Psalms 146:7-9, *NLT*).

God helps me with my fear and anxiety. "So, we say with confidence, "The Lord is my helper; I will not be afraid. What can man do to me?" (Hebrews 13:6, *NIV*).

God will never abandon or forsake me. "God has said, 'Never will I leave you; never will I forsake you'" (Hebrews 13:5, *NIV*).

I can come boldly to Christ with all my needs. "So then, since we have a great High Priest who has entered heaven, Jesus the Son of God, let us hold firmly to what we believe. This High Priest of ours understands our weaknesses, for he faced all of the same testings we do, yet he did not sin. So, let us come boldly to the throne of our gracious God. There we will receive his mercy, and we will find grace to help us when we need it most" (Hebrews 4:14-16, *NLT*).

God gives me peace. "You will keep in perfect peace all who trust in you, all whose thoughts are fixed on you!" (Isaiah 26:3, *NLT*).

God strengthens me on the inside. "I pray that out of his glorious riches he may strengthen you with power through his Spirit in your inner being" (Ephesians 3:16, *NIV*).

God comforts me. "But God, who comforts the downcast, comforted us" (2 Corinthians 7:6, *NIV*).

I live in God's presence, in His life-giving light. "You have kept my feet from slipping. So now I can walk in your presence, O God, in your life-giving light" (Psalms 56:13, *NIV*).

I can put my hope in God. "And so, Lord, where do I put my hope? My only hope is in you" (Psalms 39:7, *NLT*).

God wants to use His power in my life. "I also pray that you will understand the incredible greatness of God's power for us who believe him. This is the same mighty power that raised Christ from the dead and seated him in the place of honor at God's right hand in the heavenly realms" (Ephesians 1:19-20, *NLT*).

I can put my trust in God. "Praise the Lord! For he has heard my cry for mercy. The Lord is my strength and shield. I trust him with all my heart. He helps me, and my heart is filled with joy" (Psalms 28:6-8, *NLT*).

I can have fellowship with God. "Come close to God, and God will come close to you" (James 4:8, *NLT*).

I am chosen by God to be His ambassador of love. "So, as those who have been chosen of God, holy and beloved, put on a heart of compassion, kindness, humility, gentleness and patience; bearing with one another, and forgiving each other, whoever has a complaint against anyone; just as the Lord forgave you, so also should you" (Colossians 3:12-13, *NASB*).

I am God's prized procession. "He chose to give birth to us by giving us his true word. And we, out of all creation, became his prized possession" (James 1:18, *NLT*).

I live in forgiveness and freedom. "If we claim we have no sin, we are only fooling ourselves and not living in the truth. But if we confess our sins to him, he is faithful and just to forgive us our sins and to cleanse us from all wickedness" (1 John 1:8-9, *NLT*).

Christ's peace rules in my heart. "Let the peace of Christ rule in your hearts, since as members of one body you were called to peace. And be thankful" (Colossians 3:15, *NIV*).

I find shelter in God's presence. "You hide them in the shelter of your presence" (Psalms 31:20, *NLT*).

I will wait for Gods help. "So, the Lord must wait for you to come to him, so he can show you his love and compassion. For the Lord is a faithful God. Blessed are those who wait for his help" (Isaiah 30:15-18, *NLT*).

I am trusting God. "But I am trusting you, O Lord, saying, 'You are my God!' My future is in your hands" (Psalms 31:14-15, *NLT*).

I choose to love others. "Let us think of ways to motivate one another to acts of love and good works" (Hebrews 10:24, *NLT*).

I am loved unconditionally. "Remember me in the light of your unfailing love, for you are merciful, O Lord" (Psalms 25:7, *NLT*).

I am invited to come into the presence of our Holy God. "And so, dear brothers and sisters, we can boldly enter heaven's Most Holy Place because of the blood of Jesus. By his death, Jesus opened a new and life-giving way through the curtain into the Most Holy Place. And since we have a great High Priest who rules over God's house, let us go right into the presence of God with sincere hearts fully trusting him" (Hebrews 10:19-22, *NLT*).

I am revived by God's Word. "The instructions of the Lord are perfect, reviving the soul. The decrees of the Lord are trustworthy, making wise the simple. The commandments of the Lord are right, bringing joy to the heart. The commands of the Lord are clear, giving insight for living" (Psalms 19:7-8, *NLT*).

With God, I can. "You light a lamp for me. The Lord, my God, lights up my darkness. In your strength I can crush an army; with my God, I can scale any wall" (Psalms 18:28-29, *NLT*).

God hears my prayers. "But in my distress, I cried out to the Lord; yes, I prayed to my God for help. He heard me from his sanctuary; my cry to him reached his ears" (Psalms 18:6, *NLT*).

Acknowledgments

No one writes a book by themselves. Authors are influenced by many people and experiences that have shaped their unique story. I am no exception. This book has come out of decades of ministry and working with volunteers. It also emerges from those I have served within the exciting community of faith, beginning with my original church family, Dunning Park Chapel. Although many have gone on to be with our Savior, it was at that precious chapel that I learned to love ministry.

I give thanks to all those who participated with me in Limaland Youth for Christ in Lima, Ohio. This was the beginning of my life of ministry. We were a community of believers and had a deep love for each other, many of whom I have kept in contact with over the years.

Many thanks to the Youth group at Immanual Baptist Church in Waukegan, Illinois. They were such a precious group of young people. I learned so much working with them. So many have faithfully continued living for the Lord and are serving in various churches. Many of the principles taught in this book were used in that youth group.

I want to thank Pastor Howard Hoekstra, my Pastor at Calvary and a dear friend and co-minister. This is where I served as Executive Pastor and Pastor of Outreach for thirteen years. We were able to use many of the teachings from this book with the congregation. All my dear friends at Calvary Church, co-workers in ministry, had a tremendous influence on my life.

I thank the board members of Empower Ministry—Mary and George Van Dahm, Howard Hoekstra, and Janine Ovitt—for helping make this book become a reality. To all the donors to Empower Ministry, this book would not be produced without your financial help.

Many thanks to my twin brother Rod Ovitt for his editing and encouragement in this project. A special thanks to his wife Carolyn Ovitt for the final layout and cover art. She is truly gifted and has been an invaluable help in coordinating book branding and graphics for our book publishing.

A special thanks to Eric Swanson who was my mentor during my final year at Calvary and during the transition into starting our own ministry. He has been an inspiration and a great influence in my life toward being outwardly focused as a church.

Writing comes out of my own journey with the Lord. My own journey, of course, is with all those who I have lived and worked with. I especially want to thank my wife and three sons who shaped me during my adulthood and supported me during some of life's severe struggles. What I have learned about life from my children and grandchildren has continually inspired my writing.

Finally, my praise goes to the Lord Jesus Christ. I pray that this book will bring Him honor and praise.

OTHER BOOKS FROM THIS AUTHOR

Looking for a devotional book that speaks to your deepest needs?

MOMENT IN THE WORD
Daily Moments That Feed Your Soul

With a prolific career in both ministry and social causes, Ron Ovitt has provided a year-long collection of devotionals that will guide to praise, reflection, and worship. Different than most devotional books, *Moment in the Word* **speaks to everyday emotions and brings God's word to encourage, comfort, and console.**

Join the thousands of others who make *Moment in the Word* a part of their daily journey.

Ronald E. Ovitt, *Moment in the Word*

GILGAL
PUBLISHING

AVAILABLE ON AMAZON

OTHER BOOKS FROM THIS AUTHOR

Do you want to know about your spiritual gifts but don't know where to begin?

GIFTED
Understanding My Spiritual Gifts

Not sure what your spiritual gifts are or how to use them? Tired of surveys that leave you hanging? *Gifted* dispels the mystery around this vital topic. **Close to a million people have used these materials to research spiritual gifts.** Many have come to learn their gifts and how to put them into action. Now you can discover yours!

With a fail-safe duo-discovery method combining an online survey and individual descriptive pages on each gift, you will better understand how God has equipped you and what to do about it. Each gift description includes definition, benefits, pitfalls, ministry opportunities, and recommended further training.

Ronald E. Ovitt, *Gifted*

GILGAL
PUBLISHING

AVAILABLE ON AMAZON

OTHER BOOKS FROM THIS AUTHOR

Do you struggle with negative beliefs about yourself?

POWER UP!
Emotional Relearning™ Through Bible Verse Affirmations

Many of emotions like depression, anxiety, anger, and fear are caused by what we think and believe about ourselves. Negative lies about life and ourselves that have been emotionally believed, fill us with self-doubt and shame.

How can we rid ourselves of these negative beliefs? Now there's a way to break free from spiritual strongholds! In Power Up, **through Emotional Relearning™ you will learn how to emotionally relearn the truth and replace the negative doubts and lies that so easily bring you down with the truth about you taken directly from God's Word.** This collection of powerful Bible verses has been paraphrased into the first-person and will help you with the personal emotional battles you face each day.

Ronald E Ovitt, *Power Up!*

GILGAL
PUBLISHING

AVAILABLE ON AMAZON

OTHER BOOKS FROM THIS AUTHOR

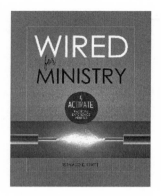

Tired of how-to information
that doesn't help you actually
begin to minister?

WIRED FOR MINISTRY
Activate your Passions, Experience, and Abilities

Now there is a tool that will help you understand how you are wired for ministry! *Wired for Ministry* holds **the secret to activating your ministry potential by discovering your spiritual gifts, ministry preferences, ministry skills, and unique ministry drive.**

This workbook culminates with the development of a *Personal Ministry Profile*, your unique "ministry resume." Presenting this to church or non-profit leaders will help them identify ministry opportunities that match your unique strengths and passions.

Used annually at Moody Bible Institute for all incoming students, this workbook can also help you learn more about your ministry potential. Activate the ministry God has inside of you!

Ronald E. Ovitt, *Wired for Ministry*

GILGAL
PUBLISHING

AVAILABLE ON AMAZON

Made in the USA
Monee, IL
08 October 2021